LOOKING AT
PHOTOGRAPHS

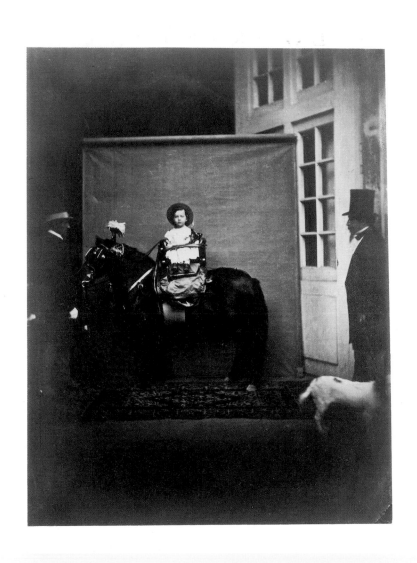

LOOKING AT
PHOTOGRAPHS

A GUIDE TO TECHNICAL TERMS

Gordon Baldwin

THE J. PAUL GETTY MUSEUM
in association with
BRITISH MUSEUM PRESS

© 1991 The J. Paul Getty Museum

Published by the
J. Paul Getty Museum
1200 Getty Center Drive
Suite 1000
Los Angeles, California 90049-1687
in association with
British Museum Press
A division of British Museum
Publications Ltd
46 Bloomsbury Street, London
WC1B 3QQ

At the J. Paul Getty Museum:
Christopher Hudson, Head of Publications
Cynthia Newman Helms, Managing Editor
Andrea P. A. Belloli, Consulting Editor
Deenie Yudell, Design Manager
Karen Schmidt, Production Manager
Leslie Holderness, Sales and
    Distribution Manager

Library of Congress Cataloguing-in-Publication Data
Baldwin, Gordon.
Looking at photographs : aguide to technical terms / Gordon Baldwin.
p. cm.
Includes bibliographical references.
ISBN 0-89236-192-1
1. Photography—Terminology.   1. Title.
TR9.B35   1991
770' .3—dc20   90-28861
                                                    CIP

British Library Cataloguing in Publication Data
Baldwin, Gordon
Looking at photographs : a guide to technical terms.
1. Photography
I. Title   II. British Museum   III. J. Paul Getty Museum
770
ISBN 0-7141-1720-X (British Museum Publications)

Second Printing

The publishers would like to acknowledge that the title *Looking at
Photographs* was first used by the Museum of Modern Art, New York,
in 1974, for a book by John Szarkowski. Mr. Szarkowski's invaluable
guide to the aesthetics of photography is wholly different from the
present glossary of technical terms.

Cover: Eugene Atget (French, 1857–1927). *Au Petit Dunkerque, 3 quai
Conti*, 1900. Albumen print showing ghost figure, 20.9 x 17.7 cm
(8⅛ x 7 in.). JPGM, 90.XM.45.1.

Frontispiece: Louis Pierson (French, 1818–1913). *Napoleon III and the
Prince Imperial*, c. 1859. Albumen print, 20.4 x 15.6 cm (8¹/₁₆ x 6⅛
in.). JPGM, 84.XM.705.

Foreword

The purpose of this book is to provide a series of concise explanations of the terms most frequently used by curators, collectors, and historians to deal with the phenomenon called photography. As this book is intended for someone actually looking at photographs, the list of terms has been limited to those likely to appear on descriptive labels in exhibitions or in catalogue entries.

From its origins at the end of the 1830s, photography has never ceased to evolve both aesthetically and technologically. For example, judging by their letters to the periodicals of the 1850s, individual photographers consistently modified both the chemical formulae and the physical manipulations required to produce negatives and prints. They also redesigned and altered their cameras and lenses. Early photographers introduced these modifications for a variety of reasons, but principally to improve the efficacy of the chemical reactions involved or to produce a variety of visual results that were governed by aesthetic choices. Today the changes occurring in photographic materials and equipment are far more likely to be the work of commercial manufacturers. In both periods, however, change has been constant. For this reason the descriptions of processes that follow are somewhat generic. When trade names have been introduced, they have been given as examples rather than recommendations.

In the writing of this book I have had the welcome advice of many friends and colleagues at the J. Paul Getty Museum, British Museum, and other institutions. I am grateful to Andrea P. A. Belloli, Robin Clark, Sheryl Conkelton, Christopher Date, Alan Donnithorne, Joan Dooley, Teresa Francis, Andee Hales, Peggy Hanssen, Kurt Hauser, Debbie Hess Norris, Judith Keller, Hope Kingsley, Craig Klyver, Brita Mack, Julia Nelson-Gel, Arthur Ollman, Charles Passela, Sandra Phillips, Ellen M. Rosenbery, Larry Schaaf, Karen Schmidt, Louise Stover, John Szarkowski, and Jay Thompson. I am particularly indebted to Weston Naef for his encouragement, to John Harris for his patience, and to Jean Smeader for both patience and paleographic expertise.

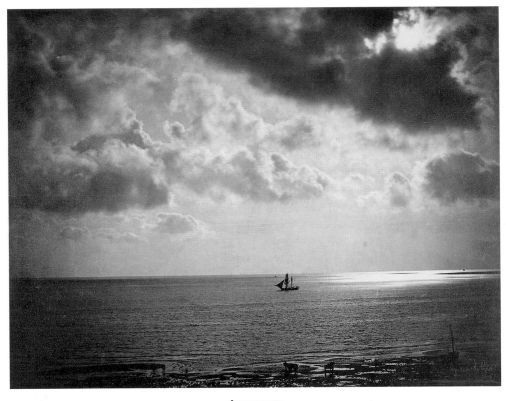

ALBUMEN PRINT

Gustave Le Gray (French, 1820–1884). *Brig on the Water*, 1856.
Albumen print, 32 × 40.8 cm (12⅝ × 16 1/16 in.). JPGM, 84.XM.637.2.

ALBUMEN PRINT

The albumen print was invented in 1850 by Louis-Desiré Blanquart-Evrard (1802–1872), and until about 1890 it was the most prevalent type of print. Normally made from a COLLODION negative on glass, it yielded a clearer image than the SALTED-PAPER print that preceded it in general use. An albumen print was made by floating a sheet of thin paper on a bath of egg white containing salt, which had been whisked, allowed to subside, and filtered. This produced a smooth surface, the pores of the paper having been filled by the albumen. After drying, the albumenized paper was sensitized by floating it on a bath of silver nitrate solution or by brushing on the same solution. The paper was again dried, but this time in the dark. (The salt and silver nitrate combined to form light-sensitive SILVER SALTS.) This doubly coated paper was put into a wooden, hinged-back frame, in contact with a negative, usually made of glass but occasionally of WAXED PAPER; it was then placed in the sun to print (see PRINTING-OUT). The progress of the printing could be checked by carefully opening the back of the frame. After printing, which sometimes required only a few minutes but could take an hour or more, the resultant proof, still unstable, was fixed by immersing it in a solution of hyposulfite of soda ("hypo") and water and then thoroughly washed to prevent further chemical reactions. The print was then dried. Variations in tone and hue were achieved by stopping the processes described above at different stages and times or, more usually, by additional TONING. (After 1855, albumen prints were almost always toned with gold chloride, which enriched their color and increased their permanence.) The finished print ranges in color from reddish to purplish brown and is usually glossy, although some early photographers preferred to reduce surface sheen by diluting the albumen with water. If an albumen print has deteriorated, its highlights are yellowish.

Note Words printed in SMALL CAPITALS refer to other entries in the book. Synonymous terms appear in parentheses; related terms are separated by a slash mark.

AMBROTYPE

(COLLODION POSITIVE)

Ambrotypes, as they are called in America, were named, it seems, after their popularizer, James Ambrose Cutting (1814–1867), who patented a specific variety of them. They are often confused with the earlier DAGUERREOTYPES, but they were made by an entirely different process, as their British name, COLLODION positives on glass, indicates. Both ambrotypes and daguerreotypes were similar in their size (small), in their packaging format (under glass in hinged cases), and in their superficial appearance (both having sharply defined images). Both were primarily used for portraiture and were unique images. An ambrotype, however, does not have the troublesome surface reflections of the daguerreotype, and its highlights are soft and pearly in tone rather than clear and crisp.

The basic process for producing an ambrotype was first published in 1851. It is an underexposed and then developed collodion negative on glass, whitish in tone, which when backed with an opaque coating (black lacquer, for example) appears as a positive image. (Where a highlight is juxtaposed to a black area, there can be a surprising discontinuity of surface caused by the dimensional difference between the image on the face of the glass plate and the black backing.)

As ambrotypes were easier to tint and faster and cheaper to make and sell than daguerreotypes, they rapidly replaced daguerreotypes in the late 1850s, only to be largely replaced in turn by TINTYPES and CARTES-DE-VISITE in the 1860s.

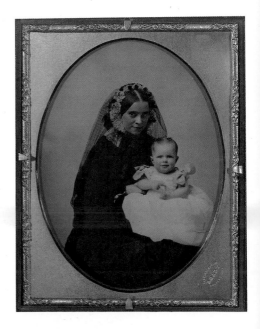

AMBROTYPE
(COLLODION POSITIVE)
Mathew Brady
(American, c. 1823–1896)
*Portrait of a Woman
and Child*, 1851
Half-plate ambrotype
with hand-coloring
12.3 × 9.1 cm
(4⅞ × 3⅝ in.)
JPGM
84.XP.447.10

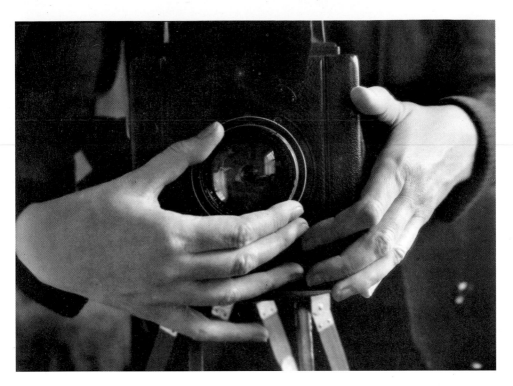

APERTURE/EXPOSURE/SHUTTER
Alma Lavenson (American, 1897–1989). *Self-Portrait*, 1932.
Gelatin silver print, 20.3 × 25.2 cm (8 × 9 ¹⁵⁄₁₆ in.). JPGM, 85.XM.283.5.

**APERTURE
/EXPOSURE
/SHUTTER**

Exposure refers to the quantity of light that falls on a negative material. In a camera, exposure is governed by the length of time the negative receives light and the size of the opening (aperture) through which the light passes. Exposure length is determined by the speed with which the shutter opens and closes, allowing light to pass through the aperture. The speed can be varied, as can the diameter of the aperture. It is the coordination of these two factors that determines optimum exposure, as both intervene between the film material and the natural or artificial light illuminating the subject.

Early cameras did not have shutters. Exposure times were so long that the photographer could manually remove and replace a cap over the lens. Today's cameras typically have electronically operated, accurate, high-speed shutters. Early aperture control was by means of a set of circular brass plates with holes of various sizes, one of which was positioned in front of, behind, or between the elements of the lens. Modern aperture controls, known as diaphragms, are highly sophisticated and are built into the lens. Aperture settings today are referred to by a numbering system known as f-stops, a ratio of the diameter of the aperture to the focal length of the lens.

ATTRIBUTION

An attribution is an authoritative statement that an unsigned photograph can be said confidently, but not definitely, to have been made by a specified photographer on the grounds of close stylistic affinity to signed works by that maker and/or other compelling circumstantial evidence.

AUTOCHROME

An autochrome is a colored transparent image on glass, similar to a slide, ranging in size from less than 2 inches (5.1 cm) square to 15 by 18 inches (38.1 by 45.7 cm). It is meant to be viewed by being held up to the light or projected onto a surface. Deeply luminous in color if unfaded, and with soft image outlines, each autochrome is a unique object.

Autochromes were the first really practicable photographs in color and were made by a process invented and patented in 1904 by Louis Lumière (1864–1948), the younger of the two brothers who figured so prominently in the invention of the motion picture. The process consisted of coating a glass plate with sticky varnish, then with a thin pressed layer of minuscule grains of translucent potato starch. The grains had been separated into three equal lots and each lot separately dyed red-orange, blue-violet, or green. Mixed together in random distribution, they formed a dense mosaic color filter on the plate. Over this layer of grains was added another coating of varnish and, finally, a gelatin-bromide emulsion that was sensitive to the entire spectrum of light, i.e., was ORTHOCHROMATIC. (The starch grain mosaic served to filter the light so that the underlying bromide emulsion was selectively exposed by color.)

Plates thus coated, which were manufactured in large quantities between 1907 and about 1940 by the Lumière brothers' company, were exposed in a camera, glass side forward, so that light entering the lens would pass through the color mosaic filter before reaching the emulsion. The plates were then developed and washed.

The resulting negatives were then placed in a chemical bath in order to bleach out the negative impression. After exposure to white light the plates were redeveloped, bringing forward a residual positive colored impression that was fixed, washed a final time, and varnished.

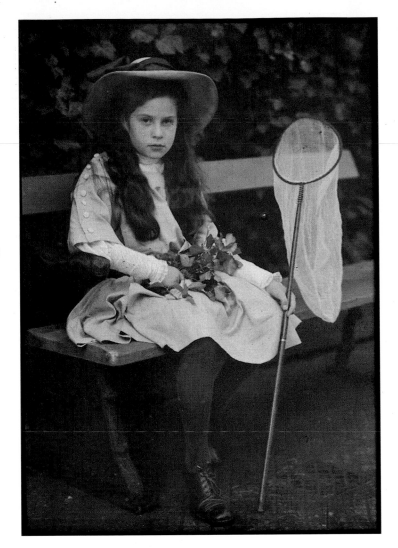

BLINDSTAMP
(DRYSTAMP)

This kind of stamp is an identification mark embossed onto the MOUNT to which a photograph has been attached. Less frequently, the blindstamp appears on the photograph itself. The stamp's raised or depressed letters usually spell the name or the address of the photographer. As no ink is used, the stamp is less visible than a WETSTAMP. Blindstamps were commonly used during the nineteenth century and are sometimes employed in modern commercial portraiture. (Illustration on page 13.)

BROMOIL PRINT
/OIL-PIGMENT PRINT

The bromoil process for making prints, which originated in England in 1907 and remained popular into the 1930s, was an outgrowth of earlier oil-pigment processes and was related to the GUM BICHROMATE process. It depended on the underlying principle of lithography, namely, that oil and water repel each other.

The process for producing a bromoil print began with a gelatin silver-bromide print, usually an enlargement from a smaller negative. This print was bleached in a solution of copper sulfate, potassium bromide, and potassium bichromate and then fixed in a solution of hyposulfite of soda ("hypo") and water. The visible image had disappeared and the gelatin had been hardened by the potassium bichromate in proportion to the amount of silver that comprised the image. The sheet, called a matrix, was soaked so that the gelatin would absorb water and was left damp. Lithographic ink or another greasy ink was then carefully and repeatedly dabbed onto the surface of the matrix with a special brush or gently applied with a rubber roller called a brayer. Where the gelatin had absorbed water (in the highlights and, to a lesser degree, in the midtones), it repelled the oil-based ink. Repeated applications of pigment gradually built up the matrix to whatever density was desired. The print thus created was either slowly dried or was used once in a press, while still wet, as a kind of printing plate to transfer the inked image to another surface. It is the combination of the original *brom*ide print and the *oil* pigment that gives the bromoil print its name.

The chosen color of the ink determined the color of the final bromoil print. (Full color was also possible by the use of three separate bromide prints for bromoil transfer, made from three negatives, each exposed through a different color filter, and three successive applications of primary colors.) The range of tones of a bromoil print is broad; its surface is not flat if it has not been transferred. Bromoil prints do not have high detail resolution, but selective brushwork permits a wide latitude of manipulation of the image.

BURNING-IN

Burning-in is a technique by which a photographer can darken the tones of a specific area of a photograph. It is used to alter highlight areas that show too little detail, i.e., are too light in tone, or for dark areas that are too light. The photographer usually decides to employ burning-in after examining the negative, a contact sheet, or, more likely, an enlarged trial print from the negative. The technique is most often used during enlargement and consists of interposing for part of the exposure a piece of cardboard, plastic, or the like, with a hole cut out in its center, between the beam of light coming through the negative via the

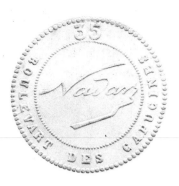

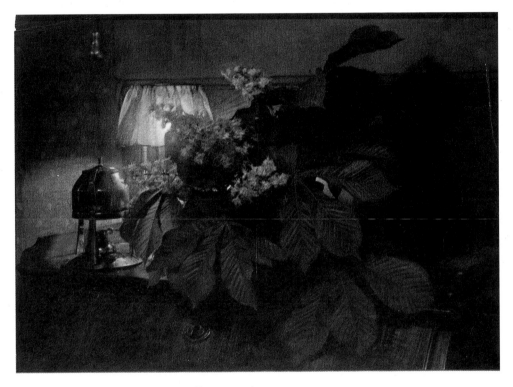

BROMOIL PRINT/OIL-PIGMENT PRINT

Heinrich Kühn (German, 1866–1944). *Still Life with Flowers, Lamp, and Urn*, c. 1905.
Bromoil transfer print, 33.5×45.8 cm (13³⁄₁₆×18¼ in.). JPGM, 84.XM.829.5.

CABINET CARD
Gagen and Fraser
(Canadian, active 1880s)
*Portrait of a Canadian
Couple,* c. 1885
Albumen print
cabinet card
recto and verso
16.5 × 10.7 cm
(6½ × 4¼ in.)
JPGM
84.XD.879.0149

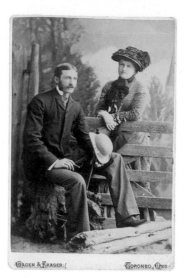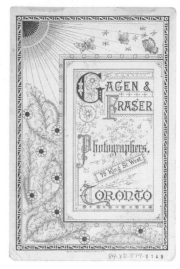

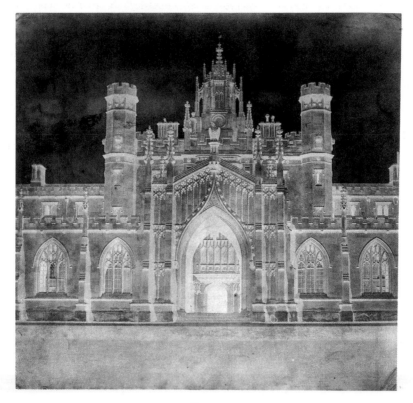

CALOTYPE
(TALBOTYPE)
William Henry Fox Talbot (British, 1800–1877). *New Court, St. John's College, Cambridge,* c. 1845.
Waxed calotype negative, 16.8 × 16.9 cm (6⅝ × 6¹¹/₁₆ in.). JPGM, 84.XM.1002.5.

enlarging lens and the print being made. The unshaded area receives more light and hence darkens, which gives more detail in highlight areas. To avoid creating a sharp shadow outline, the photographer moves the cardboard back and forth. Depending on the shape and size of the area to be darkened, holes or silhouettes of various kinds can be cut in the cardboard. The photographer can also use his or her cupped hands or fingers to shade the print. If a photographer uses burning-in while contact-printing, she or he interposes the instrument between the light source and the negative. For a related technique, see DODGING.

CABINET CARD

A cabinet card, larger in scale and later in date than a CARTE-DE-VISITE, was a stiff piece of thick cardstock, about 6¼ by 4¼ inches (15.9 by 10.8 cm), bearing on one side a photograph of somewhat smaller dimensions. Initially the photograph was nearly always an ALBUMEN print (but later was a GELATIN SILVER or CARBON print) and was most often a bust-length portrait made in a studio, although views were also popular. The balance of the space on the card's face at top or bottom was usually printed or embossed with the photographer's name or insignia and occasionally with the name of the sitter. Often the back also bore the photographer's imprint. Introduced in the 1860s, cabinet cards gradually superseded the flimsier and smaller cartes-de-visite in the public's favor. Their popularity waned in the 1890s, particularly after the introduction of scenic view postcards and enlarged studio portraits.

CALOTYPE
(TALBOTYPE)

William Henry Fox Talbot's calotype process for the making of paper negatives, which he discovered in 1840 and patented in 1841, was the direct ancestor of modern photography as it was a process that involved both a NEGATIVE and a POSITIVE. Unlike the DAGUERREOTYPE, which was a unique object, the calotype depended on the creation of a negative that could be used for making multiple prints. These were usually SALT prints. The calotype was a significant advance over Talbot's earlier PHOTO-GENIC DRAWING process, as he used chemicals that were more light sensitive and the negative image was completed by DEVELOPMENT rather than PRINTING-OUT.

A calotype was made by brushing a silver-nitrate solution onto one side of a sheet of high-quality writing paper and drying it. Then, by candlelight, the sheet was floated on a potassium iodide solution, producing slightly light-sensitive silver iodide. The sheet was dried again, this time in the dark. Shortly before exposure in a camera, the paper was, in weak light, again swabbed with silver nitrate, this time mixed with acetic and gallic acids, thus producing genuine light sensitivity. This sensitized sheet could be used damp in the camera, where an exposure of ten seconds to ten minutes was necessary, depending on the weather, time of day, intensity of the chemicals employed, and subject. At this point the image was not visible but latent in the paper. To develop the image, the sheet was again dipped in a bath of silver nitrate and acetic and gallic acids. To fix the negative image, now wholly visible, on the paper, Talbot washed the paper in water, then bathed it with a solution of bromide of potassium. He then washed the paper in water again and dried it. Soon after his announcement of this method, Talbot, at Sir John Herschel's suggestion, amended its final steps by fixing the image with hyposulfite of soda ("hypo"), a chemical used for the fixing of prints to this day but now correctly known as sodium thiosulfate. The negative thus produced could then be used for the printing of positive proofs, although its transparency could be improved by waxing. As the image was contained in the paper, having soaked into it, so to speak (rather than carried on a completely transparent medium like glass), the paper fibers tended to show through to the proof, causing a relative lack of clarity in the details and an overall subtle mottling of tones. The process, with various modifications, was popular from 1841 until the early 1850s, when it was superseded by the WET-COLLODION-on-glass process. It enjoyed a revival about 1900 by the Pictorialist photographers, who valued the light-diffusing effect created by the paper fiber.

The word *calotype* has sometimes also been used to refer to the SALTED-PAPER prints made from calotype negatives, as well as the negatives themselves. Talbot used it for negatives, and it seems simpler to reserve the word for the negative alone unless the print is definitely known to have been developed out rather than printed out. Before 1850, the negatives were admired as objects in their own right, and negatives of that period are occasionally exhibited as such today. Talbot coined the word *calotype* from the Greek *kalos*, meaning beautiful, and the Latin *typus*, meaning image.

CAMERA

The nearly universal means for making a photograph is the camera, which basically consists of a lightproof compartment with, on one side, a lens that can be closed and through which the subject can be focused and, on another side, a flat, light-sensitive material, whether film or plate, on which the image can be received. Cameras have undergone nearly infinite permutations, from William Henry Fox Talbot's tiny wooden boxes of the mid-1830s to the electronic marvels of the present. The name comes from the Latin for room, which a camera does resemble.

CAMERA LUCIDA

Invented in 1806 and somewhat oddly named by William Hyde Wollaston (1766–1828), the camera lucida (Latin, meaning lighted room) was an apparatus to aid a draftsman in rendering a view. It consisted of a prism with three or four sides atop a vertical rod, with a clamp at the bottom to mount it to a drafting board or pad. The draftsman directed the prism's vertical side toward the desired view and looked down with one eye, through *and* past the prism's horizontal edge, to the paper below. By the action of the eye, the view reflected through the prism seemed to merge with the paper surface below, so that the view appeared to be *on* the paper. The draftsman could then trace this image. Camera lucidas were awkward to use, and it was William Henry Fox Talbot's discontent with this tool, he said, that led him to invent the process that evolved into modern photography. Although tricky to master, a camera lucida was more easily portable than its predecessor, the CAMERA OBSCURA.

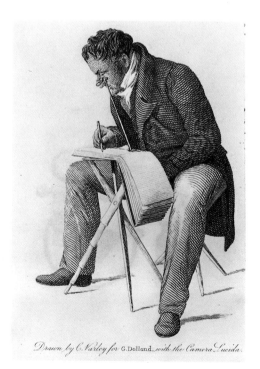

CAMERA LUCIDA
Cornelius Varley
(British, 1781–1873)
*Artist Sketching with
a Wollaston-Style
Camera Lucida,* c. 1830
Engraving
16.5 × 7.5 cm
(6 ½ × 2 ¹⁵⁄₁₆ in.)
Gernsheim Collection
Harry Ransom
Humanities Research
Center
The University of Texas
at Austin

Drawn by C. Varley for G. Dolland, *with the Camera Lucida.*

From the Latin meaning dark chamber, the camera obscura was an ancestor of the modern camera. The principle that light rays travel in straight lines has been known since antiquity. As early as the ninth century it was observed that when light rays from a bright object enter a small hole in a darkened room, they produce an inverted image of that object on the opposite wall. By the seventeenth century this observation had led to the creation of a portable camera obscura as an aid for drawing, a use Giovanni Battista Della Porta had first suggested a century earlier.

A simple form of this draftsman's apparatus consisted of an oblong closed box fitted at one end with a lens that could be adjusted to focus on an image. Inside the box, at the other end, a mirror was attached at a forty-five-degree angle, and this mirror projected the image up onto a ground-glass screen that had been set into the top of the box. It was on this ground-glass screen that the image could then be traced on thin paper by the draftsman. (The mirror also served to reverse the image, which had been inverted as it passed through the lens. Thus, the image traced by the draftsman was a "true" image, having been re-reversed by the mirror.) In this way, a view in three dimensions was converted to two dimensions, facilitating the draftsman's task.

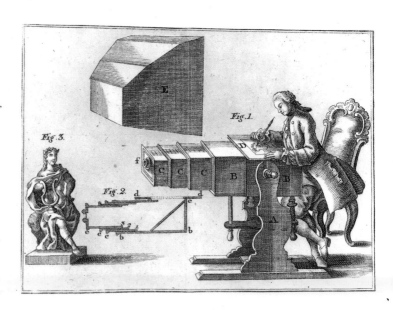

CAMERA OBSCURA
Georg Brander
(German, 1713–1783)
Table Camera Lucida, 1769,
showing cross section
with mirror
Engraving
12 × 16 cm
(4¾ × 6³⁄₁₆ in.)
Gernsheim Collection
Harry Ransom
Humanities Research
Center
The University of Texas
at Austin

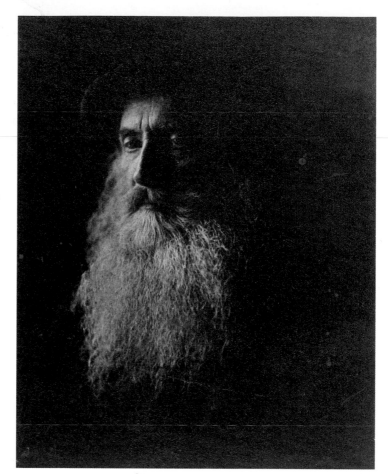

CARBON PRINT

Although patented in 1855 by Alphonse Louis Poitevin (1819–1882) and improved in 1858 by John Pouncy (1818–1894), carbon prints only became fully practicable in 1864, with the patented process and printing papers of Joseph Wilson Swan (1828–1914). The primary importance of a carbon print is its permanence, as it contains no silver impurities that can deteriorate. The process's underlying principle is the fact that gelatin to which potassium bichromate has been added becomes insoluble when exposed to light, in proportion to the amount of light received.

Basically the process worked as follows. A sheet of lightweight paper, often referred to as tissue, was coated with gelatin containing potassium bichromate and a pigment, usually the carbon black that gives the process its name. In daylight this tissue was placed under and in contact with a negative. This exposure was timed, as the dark-colored paper did not show an emerging image. Those parts of the gelatin that were exposed to light through the negative hardened. In order to wash away the unhardened gelatin and reveal the image, the face of the exposed carbon tissue was squeezed in contact with a second sheet of paper coated with an insoluble gelatin layer, thus forming a sort of gelatin sandwich; this sandwich was then soaked in warm water. The original paper floated free, or was peeled away, and the unhardened gelatin was washed away, leaving the image attached to the second sheet. (This transfer was necessary as the originally exposed sheet had a topmost, impermeable film of hardened gelatin, so that when soaked, the relatively soft layer of gelatin, in contact with the paper itself, would have caused the whole of the gelatin layer to lift up from its support.) The sheet was then immersed in water containing alum. The alum further hardened the remaining gelatin and removed any yellowish bichromate stains. Because of the transfer to a second sheet of paper, the finished image was reversed (as it was in early daguerreotypes). This effect could be counteracted by either reversing the negative at the outset or by a second reversing transfer at the end. In some instances, however, photographers were content to leave the image reversed.

Popular between 1870 and 1910, carbon prints exhibit dense glossy darks, either black or a deep rich brown in color. A wide variety of colors was possible with the use of various pigments. The prints have slight relief contours, thickest in the darkest areas where more pigmented gelatin remains. Carbon prints are occasionally made today, sometimes by means of the patented Fresson process.

CARBRO PRINT

The carbro print process of about 1919 is an outgrowth of the earlier CARBON-PRINT process of the 1860s and led via the ozotype and ozobrome processes to the color carbro process. A monochrome carbro print begins with a finished GELATIN SILVER-BROMIDE print, which is a print made on paper bearing a highly light-sensitive silver-bromide emulsion. This print, when wet, is pressed together with a sensitized carbro tissue. The tissue is a thin paper coated with pigmented gelatin that has first been sensitized by immersion in a solution of potassium bichromate and then immersed in a bath containing bleaching agents. Through chemical action, the gelatin of the carbro tissue hardens in proportion to the selective bleaching out of the silver of the bromide print. The print and the tissue are separated and the tissue placed face down on a sheet of transfer paper for about twenty minutes. The tissue and transfer paper are then separated in warm water, leaving the gelatin layer attached to the transfer paper. The paper is then bathed until the excess softened gelatin is washed away, leaving the partially hardened gelatin image. The print is further hardened in an alum bath; then it is dried. As it is silver-free, the monochrome image thus produced is permanent, that is, it does not fade. The original bromide print, now bleached, can be redeveloped and used to make as many as five additional carbro prints.

Tricolor carbro prints are made possible by a further evolution of the process, in which three bromide prints of one subject are used. The negatives for these prints are made by photographing the subject or a color image of the subject through a red, a green, and a blue filter. From these "separation negatives" the bromide prints are made. Each is then placed in contact with a thin bichromated gelatin tissue, pigmented in accordance with the color of the filter used on the negative. The process continues as described above, and the resultant three transfer papers, each carrying a different color, are stacked together in careful alignment, that is,

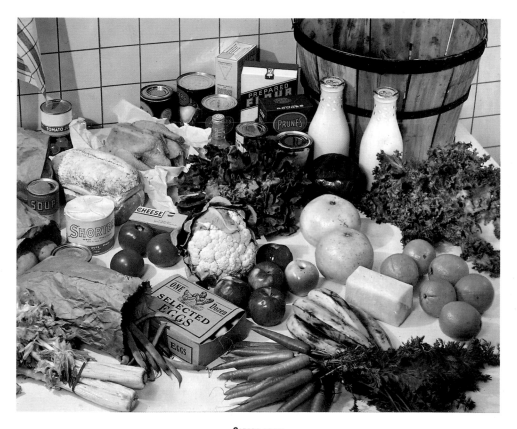

CARBRO PRINT
Paul Outerbridge (American, 1896–1958). *Food Display*, 1937.
Tricolor carbro print, 36.2 × 44.3 cm (14¼ × 17⁷⁄₁₆ in.). JPGM, 87.XM.66.4.

in registration, to produce a single colored image. Like a black-and-white carbro print, this image is permanent. The name *carbro* comes from *car*bon and *bro*mide. The process has been in use since the early twentieth century (although its use now is rare). See also DYE TRANSFER.

CARD PHOTOGRAPH   This terms applies to any of the standard-sized nineteenth-century commercially formatted photographs mounted to cards of various weights. Most successful were the midsized CARTE-DE-VISITE and CABINET CARD, but card photographs also included, in ascending order, the Trilby (about 2 by 2¾ inches [5.1 by 7 cm]), Victoria, Promenade, Boudoir, and Imperial (about 7 by 10 inches [17.8 by 25.4 cm]).

CARTE-DE-VISITE   A carte-de-visite is a stiff piece of card measuring about 4½ by 2½ inches (11.4 by 6.4 cm), the size of a formal visiting card of the 1850s (hence the name), with an attached photograph of nearly the same size. Patented in 1854 by A. A. E. Disderi (1819–1889) and popularized by him in the following decade, cartes normally bore carefully posed full-length studio portraits, often of celebrities. They were nearly always ALBUMEN prints from WET-COLLODION-on-glass negatives. Cartes-de-visite were made by the millions worldwide during the 1860s and were often collected in albums for home perusal. When they were not portraits, their subjects were often scenic views, tourist attractions, local inhabitants, or reproductions of works of art. The backs normally were printed with the photographer's name and address and, sometimes, insignia. They were gradually replaced in the public's esteem by the CABINET CARD during the late 1870s.

CASED PHOTOGRAPH   A cased photograph, nearly always a DAGUERREOTYPE or AMBROTYPE, is a photograph that has been secured, usually by its maker, inside a shallow hinged case for its safekeeping or display. Cases were widely available commercially from the early 1840s to give additional protection to daguerreotypes, which as a matter of course had glass coverings over their image surfaces.

The three principal kinds of cases were thin, embossed, leather-covered, lidded wooden boxes; papier-mâché cases; and molded and lidded boxes made of thermoplastic (pressed, pigmented sawdust and shellac), with embossed decorative elements, usually called "Union cases." All three kinds were only slightly larger than the daguerreotypes they contained. They were usually lined with

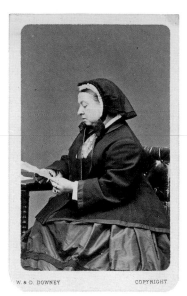
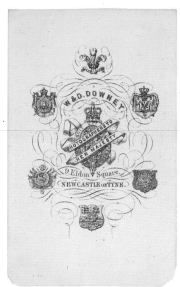

CARTE-DE-VISITE
William and Daniel
Downey
(British, active c. 1860–
early 1900s)
Queen Victoria, c. 1880
Albumen print
carte-de-visite
recto and verso
10.3 × 6.3 cm
(4⅛ × 2½ in.)
JPGM
84.XD.737.271

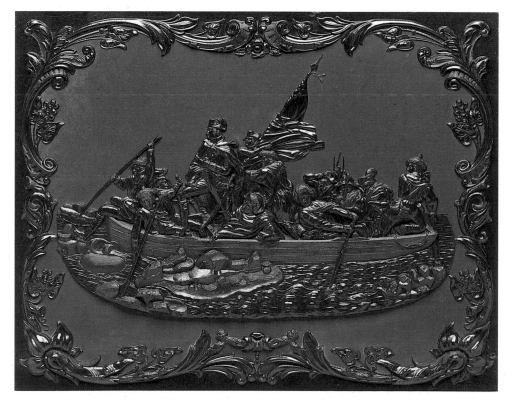

CASED PHOTOGRAPH
Thermoplastic wholeplate daguerreotype case manufactured by Littlefield, Parsons and Company, 1858.
Lid with image molded from a die engraving by Frederick B. Smith and Herman Hartmann adapted from
Emanuel Leutze's painting *Washington Crossing the Delaware*, 18.3 × 23.4 cm (7¼ × 9¼ in.). JPGM, 84.XT.1568.2.

velvet or silk that sometimes was imprinted with the photographer's name.

The daguerreotype, cover glass, and brass mat were held together with a paper seal and enclosed by a thin brass outer frame, called a preserver. This unit was inserted into the case.

CHROMOGENIC PRINT

A chromogenic print is a color print made from a color transparency or negative, in which the print material has at least three emulsion layers of SILVER SALTS (halides). Each of the three layers is sensitized to one of the three primary colors of light: blue, green, and red. Thus, each layer records different information about the color make-up of the image. (The red layer "remembers" red, and so on.) During exposure to the negative, a colorless silver image is formed in each layer. After initial development of the silver images, further development follows in several steps in which chemical compounds (dye couplers) are added that unite with the products of the silver development to form dyes of the appropriate colors in the emulsion layers. When seen against the white base of the print stock, the layers appear as a single image in full color. The remaining silver is bleached and then dissolved out in the FIXING process. The entire process is somewhat different if a color transparency rather than a negative is present at the outset. Chromogenic (from the Greek, meaning color-forming) prints, of which Ektachrome is an example, have various resis-

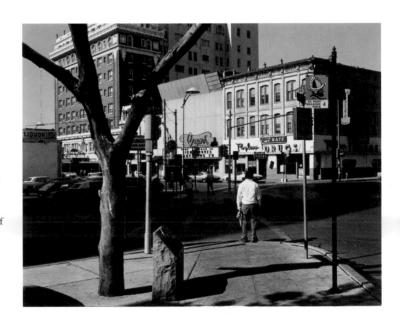

CHROMOGENIC PRINT
Stephen Shore
(American, b. 1947)
El Paso, Street, 1975
Chromogenic print
(Ektacolor contact print)
20×24.8 cm
(7⅞×9¾ in.)
San Francisco Museum of
Modern Art
86.201

tances to fading or staining from residual chemical impurities, depending on their specific manufacture. They are not as stable as DYE DESTRUCTION or DYE TRANSFER prints.

The French term *cliché verre* (meaning glass negative) denotes a particular use of glass as a negative for a drawing. The glass plate can be prepared in either of two ways. The more common method is to cover the plate with an opaque ground, like paint or smoke, and then draw with a pointed instrument on it, scratching through to the glass, much like preparing an etching plate for biting in acid. The plate is then used as a negative and CONTACT PRINTED or ENLARGED onto a sheet of light-sensitive paper. The print thus produced is a design of dark lines on a white background. The alternate method is to draw with paint or another medium on uncoated glass. This, when used as a negative, produces a print with white lines on a dark ground. William Henry Fox Talbot employed this process as early as 1835, and it continues to be used occasionally.

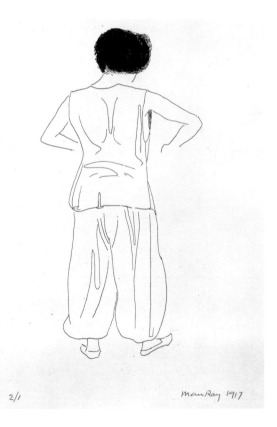

CLICHÉ VERRE
Man Ray
(American, 1890–1976)
Figure in Harem Pants
1917
Gelatin silver cliché verre
17.3 × 12.2 cm
(6¹³⁄₁₆ × 4¹³⁄₁₆ in.)
JPGM
84.XM.1000.107

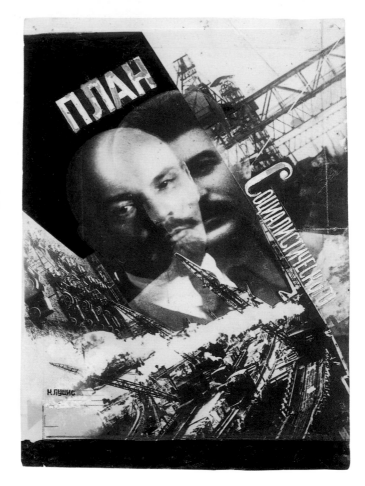

**COLLAGE
/MONTAGE**

Collage (from the French *coller*, to glue) is the combination on a common support of diverse fragments of various materials. These can be photographic or not, with or without specific image content. There is normally no attempt to conceal the edges of the parts, which may be roughly torn or smoothly cut, and there may be considerable handwork in pencil, pen, or brush on the surface. The artistic result relies in part on juxtaposition and texture and often tends to the abstract.

Montage (from the French *monter*, to mount) is the combination of diverse photographic images to produce a new work. The combination is often achieved by rephotographing the mounted elements or by multiple darkroom exposures. In the finished work, the actual physical edges become inconspicuous. The artistic result often tends to the surreal rather than the abstract.

Both photomontage and collage originated shortly before 1920, and the two are not always differentiated.

In the nineteenth century, the collodion used to coat glass plates was made from gun cotton, a commercially available product, which was ordinary cotton that had been soaked in nitric and sulfuric acid and then dried. The photographer dissolved gun cotton in a mixture of alcohol and ether to which potassium iodide had been added. The resultant collodion was a syrupy mixture that could be poured onto clean glass plates as the first step in the production of negatives.

The wet-collodion process was invented in 1848 by F. Scott Archer (1813–1857) and published by him in 1851. It was prevalent from 1855 to about 1881, gradually displacing both the DAGUERREO-TYPE and CALOTYPE processes. Wet-collodion-on-glass negatives were valued because the transparency of the glass produced a high resolution of detail in both the highlights and shadows of the resultant prints and because exposure times were shorter than those for the daguerreotype or calotype, ranging from a few seconds to a few minutes, depending on the amount of light available. Finished negatives were usually used to produce ALBU-MEN prints, although SALT prints were sometimes made during the 1850s and early 1860s.

In the wet-collodion process, collodion was poured from a beaker with one hand onto a perfectly cleaned GLASS PLATE, which was continuously and steadily tilted with the other hand, to quickly produce an even coating. (The plate was of whatever size the finished print was to be, from a quarter plate measuring 4 by 5 inches [10.2 by 12.7 cm] to a mammoth plate measuring 18 by 21 inches [35.7 by 53.3 cm].) When the collodion had set but not dried (a matter of some seconds), the plate was sensitized by bathing it in a solution of silver nitrate, which combined with the potassium iodide in the collodion to produce light-sensitive silver iodide. The plate in its holder was then placed in a camera for exposure while still wet—hence the name of the process. After exposure, the plate was immediately developed in a solution of pyrogallic and acetic acids; a later refinement of the process used ferrous sulfate as a developer.

As some of these steps required darkness, photographers had to take dark tents or wagons as well as chemicals and glass plates into the field with them. When enough detail became visible in the negative in the weak light of a darkroom, the negative was removed from the developer, washed in water, fixed with a solution of sodium thiosulfate to remove excess undeveloped silver iodide, and thoroughly washed to remove the sodium thiosulfite, and dried. With the addition of a protective coat of varnish, the negative was ready to be used to make prints. That this complicated process was often used in remote places by

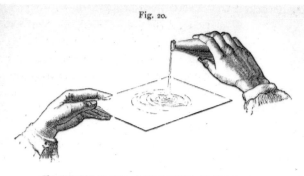

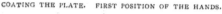

COATING THE PLATE. FIRST POSITION OF THE HANDS.

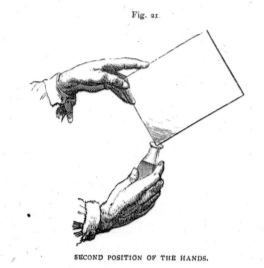

SECOND POSITION OF THE HANDS.

COLLODION/WET-COLLODION
PROCESS
Coating a glass plate and
draining the excess
collodion.
Woodcut from
Gaston Tissandier's
A History and Handbook of
Photography
(New York, 1877)

nineteenth-century photographers is a testimony to their diligence and dedication to their craft.

The dry-collodion process, of which there were several types from the mid-1850s to the mid-1860s, was a variant of the wet-collodion process that made chemical manipulations unnecessary immediately before the exposure of the plate. These processes fundamentally consisted of an additional coating of the sensitized plate with an ingredient that kept the collodion slightly moist and thereby extended the time the plate remained light-sensitive; albumen, honey, gelatin, resin, raspberry syrup (!), and beer were among the substances employed. Inconsistent results and exposure times up to six times as long as those required for wet collodion meant that dry-collodion plates never became widely popular.

COLLODION POSITIVE   See AMBROTYPE.

COLLOTYPE

The collotype (from the Greek *kollo*, meaning glue) is a kind of PHOTOLITHOGRAPH in which glass replaces stone as the printing surface. In its gradual evolution from the work of Alphonse Louis Poitevin (1819–1882) in the 1850s, the collotype has had a variety of names given to it by its developers, among them the Albertype, Lichtdruck, phototype or phototypie, heliotype, and artotype. It is still in occasional use.

The collotype is a photomechanically produced printed image, which can be of very high quality, made from a photographic image. Its production calls for a glass plate to be coated with a base layer of gelatin hardened with sodium silicate and a second layer of gelatin rendered sensitive to light by the addition of potassium or ammonium bichromate. The doubly coated plate is then dried in a darkened oven at low heat. The plate is exposed to light (that is, CONTACT PRINTED) under a negative of the desired image. In proportion to the amount of light received, the second level of gelatin hardens. When the exposed plate is thoroughly

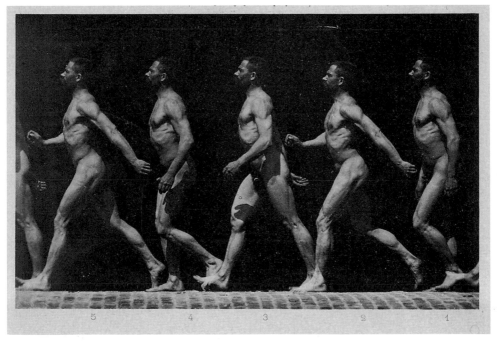

COLLOTYPE
Etienne-Jules Marey (French, 1830–1904). Detail of *La marche*, plate 6 from *Études de physiologie artistique*, 1893.
Collotype from a negative of c. 1890, 11.3 × 17.7 cm (4½ × 7 in.). JPGM, 84.XP.960.63.

washed in water, excess bichromate runs off and the gelatin swells and buckles, producing a very finely veined pattern of wrinkles called reticulation: valleys of hardened gelatin separated by bumps with the capacity to absorb water.

Next, the plate is treated with a glycerine solution that promotes further absorption of water by the bumps between the veins. Then the plate is dampened and carefully rolled with ink. As in a lithographic process, the greasy ink is repulsed from the water-swollen bumps but adheres along the lines of reticulation. The inked plate is then printed on paper, producing a finely detailed image with considerable subtlety of tone in the grays and the appearance of having continuous tone. The pattern of reticulation is visible only under high magnification; for this reason, a finished collotype, particularly if varnished, is often difficult to distinguish from a true photograph.

COMBINATION PRINT   The combining of two or more negatives into a single print during the printing process results in a combination print. Its

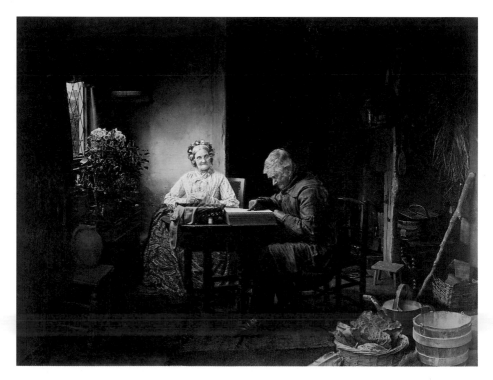

COMBINATION PRINT
Henry Peach Robinson (British, 1830–1901). *When the Day's Work Is Done*, 1877. Albumen print from six negatives, 56.2 × 74.1 cm (22⅛ × 29⅛ in.). JPGM, 84.XM.898.1.

normal means of production begins with masking part of a negative when exposing the printing paper under it and then re-exposing that paper under another partially masked negative, this time with the part of the print covered that had initially been exposed. Careful alignment, called registration, is necessary to produce a single, seamless image. The technique was used principally for landscapes, especially during the 1850s, when the oversensitivity of COLLODION to blue light made it difficult to obtain a single negative that rendered both sky and landscape. Combination prints were also used in portraiture: with this technique, the photographer could place the sitter in a setting different from the one in which the photograph was actually made. Another means of accomplishing a somewhat similar end was to print two negatives together simultaneously. From a specially prepared negative, the appearance of falling snow could thus be added to an image taken in midsummer. A combination print is not to be confused with a DOUBLE EXPOSURE.

CONTACT PRINT

Made in direct contact with a negative of whatever material, a contact print is necessarily of the same dimensions as the negative. Most nineteenth-century prints were contact prints; most modern prints are ENLARGEMENTS.

CRACKLURE
(CRAQUELURE)

These terms (one English, the other French) refer to a network of tiny cracks on a surface caused by the shrinkage of a covering layer from its support. They are used to describe the deteriorated surfaces of some ALBUMEN prints, CARBON prints, GELATIN SILVER prints, and COLLODION-on-glass negatives.

CROPPING
(TRIMMING)

Cropping is the alteration of what appears in the negative of a photograph in order to change the proportions or dimensions of a print made from that negative. Often employed to edit out peripheral detail, cropping can be accomplished by physically cutting the edges of a print or by blocking the edges of the negative in the enlarging or printing processes. Unless another uncropped print or the negative itself is known, cropping is undetectable, although it can sometimes be deduced from a print's unusual proportions. (Illustration on next page.)

CYANOTYPE

The cyanotype process for making prints was invented by Sir John Herschel in 1842 and derived from his recognition of the light sensitivity of iron salts. A sheet of paper is brushed with solutions of ferric ammonium citrate and potassium ferricyanide and dried in the dark. The object to be reproduced, be it a drawing, negative, or plant specimen, is then placed upon the sensitized sheet in direct sunlight. After about a fifteen-minute exposure, an impression has been formed, white where the light has not penetrated, on a blue ground. The paper is then washed in water, where oxidation produces the brilliant blue (cyan) that gives the process its name. A variant of this blueprint process was used for years to duplicate architects' drawings.

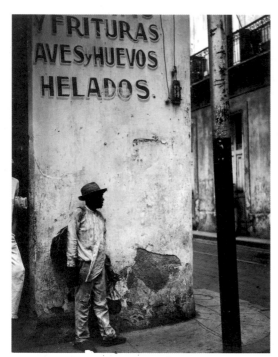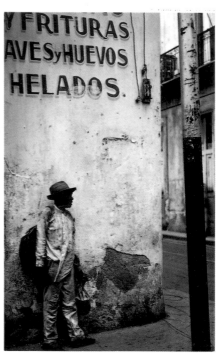

CROPPING (TRIMMING)
Walker Evans (American, 1903–1975). *Boy at Havana Corner*, 1933.
Gelatin silver print, 20 × 15.2 cm (7⅞ × 5³¹/₃₂ in.). JPGM, 84.XM.956.262.
Havana Corner, 1933. Gelatin silver print,
19.6 × 12.3 cm (7¾ × 4⅞ in.). JPGM, 84.XM.956.168.

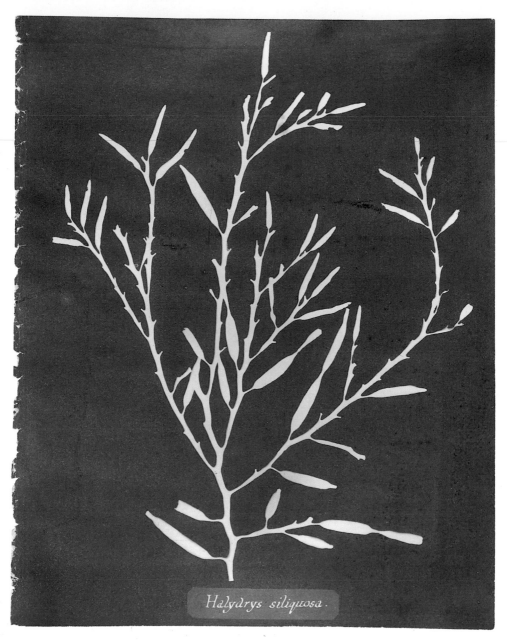

Halydrys siliquosa.

CYANOTYPE

Anna Atkins (British, 1799–1871). *Halydrys Siliquosa*, plate 19 from volume 1 of
Photographs of British Algae, 1843/44.
Cyanotype, 12.5 × 10 cm (4 ¹⁵/₁₀ × 4 in.). British Library.

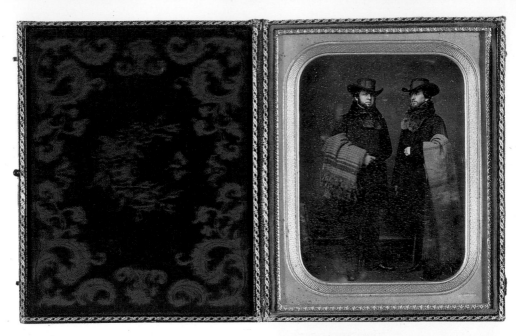

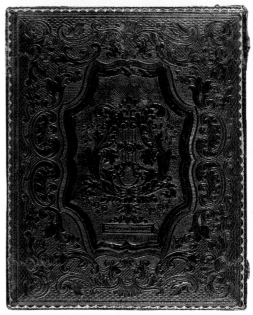

DAGUERREOTYPE
John Frederick Polycarpus
von Schneidau
(American,
b. Sweden, 1812–1855)
Two Travelers, 1852–1855
Half-plate daguerreotype
image (inside mat)
11.4 × 8.3 cm
(4½ × 3³⁄₁₆ in.)
Case (closed), 15 × 12 cm
(6 × 4¾ in.)
JPGM
84.XT.1565.29 and
outside cover

DAGUERREOTYPE

A daguerreotype is a highly detailed image formed on a sheet of copper very thinly plated with silver. Extremely thorough, even exhaustive cleaning and polishing of the silver was the first essential step in the making of a daguerreotype. Next came the suspension of the shiny plate over iodine in a closed container. Rising vapors from the iodine united with the silver to produce a light-sensitive surface coating of silver iodide. The sensitized plate, inside a lightproof holder, was then transferred to a camera and, in the earliest days, exposed to light for as long as twenty-five minutes. The plate was developed by placing it in a container suspended over a heated dish of mercury, the vapor from which reacted with the exposed silver iodide to produce an image in an amalgam of silver mercury. The image was made permanent, i.e., FIXED, by immersion in a solution of salt or hyposulfite of soda and toned with gold chloride to improve its color, definition, and permanence. The image thus produced had startling clarity.

Daguerreotypes were highly vulnerable to physical damage from abrasion and chemical damage from tarnishing. Therefore, they were normally protected by a metal mat and a covering sheet of glass, which were sealed with tape and fitted into a booklike case made of wood-covered leather or primitive plastic (compressed sawdust and resin) and lined with dark velvet (see CASED PHOTOGRAPH). As the image lies on the surface of a highly polished plate, to be seen it must be held at an angle to minimize reflections. The shadows in a daguerreotype appear to recede, creating an illusion of depth. The earliest daguerreotypes have laterally reversed images, as in a mirror; later, to correct this reversal, an actual mirror was placed at an angle in front of the lens when the exposure was made and the reflection of the subject was then photographed.

The announcement in 1839 of the invention of this process by Louis-Jacques-Mandé Daguerre (1787–1851), who had appropriated the research of Nicéphore Niépce (1765–1833), was widely acclaimed. Refinements of technique and equipment, which followed immediately, considerably reduced exposure times and made the daguerreotype wildly popular as a medium for portraiture until the middle of the 1850s, even though it was not inexpensive. Its grayish white tones were often modified by the delicate application of color, heightening the apparent realism of the portrait.

DARKROOM

(DARK CHAMBER)

Because of the light-sensitive properties inherent in photographic materials, a darkened enclosure has always been necessary for a photographer, whether for the initial sensitizing of the negative material (which was done by the photographer in the early years of photography) or for the development of the negative or the printing of proofs. Such enclosures have taken many forms, from modern-day darkrooms to the nineteenth-century traveling photographer's portable tent or van. The essential components of darkrooms have varied with the changing nature of photographic processes.

DENSITY

The technical term *density*, when applied to a photographic print or negative, indicates a precise measurement of the amount of light reflected from or absorbed by a particular area of a photograph or, in the case of a negative, transmitted through an area of that negative. Density depends on the amount of silver deposited in a specific area of a photograph at the end of the photographic process, and it determines the work's depth of tones. In the nineteenth century, density was inexactly measured by eye. Today such measurements can be made by using an electronic machine called a densitometer, first proposed jointly in 1890 by Ferdinand Hurter (1844–1898) and Vero Charles Driffield (1848–1915). By recording the depths of tone at a series of points on the print before and after exhibition, one can determine if prolonged exposure to gallery lighting has altered a photograph. Calculations of the densities of negatives are also used by photographers to determine optimum exposure times for prints to be made from a particular negative.

DEPTH OF FIELD

In describing a photograph, depth of field refers to the extent to which the space surrounding a subject appears to be sharply defined, both the space beyond the subject and between the subject and the camera. If foreground, middle ground, and background all seem to be in focus, the work can be said to have great depth of field. Technically, depth of field is dependent on the focal length of the camera lens, the size of the camera APER-TURE, and the distance of the camera from the subject.

Developing-out paper   These are papers designed for the production of photographic prints from negatives by chemical development rather than by the action of light alone (see PRINTING-OUT paper). Developing-out papers for enlargement using artificial light are coated with a silver-bromide emulsion, usually made of gelatin, that is highly sensitive to light. Developing-out papers for CONTACT PRINTING by artificial light carry a silver-chloride emulsion. (During the gaslight era, this second kind of developing paper was sometimes called gaslight paper because it could be prepared in dim gaslight, exposed in full gaslight, and developed in dim.) Both types are briefly exposed to light under a negative and then chemically developed to produce an image. Developing-out papers were available from 1873 onward; having been substantially improved by 1880, they became popular, and after 1900 they were preeminent. They were the ancestors of modern GELATIN SILVER photographic papers. The images produced are cool in tone unless altered by chemical TONING.

Development   This basic step in the production of a photograph began with Talbot's discovery in 1840 that after exposure in a camera, a negative contained an invisible or latent image that could be chemically transformed into a visible image. Development is thus the immersion of the negative in a bath containing specific chemicals for each kind of negative material in order to bring forth the visible image. This process is delicate, requiring careful control of light, chemicals, temperature, and time. An analogous process is used for the production of prints from the negative. It is during the development process that the exposed silver halides are transformed into the metallic silver that comprises the final image of most black-and-white photographs. Development is followed by FIXING and WASHING.

Digital image   As the rod and cone photoreceptors of the human eye enable it to form an image and as light-sensitive SILVER SALTS produce a photographic image in a camera, so a gridded mosaic of light-sensitive picture elements, called pixels, embedded on a computer chip permits the generation of digital images. By means of a transducer, the pixels emit electrical signals proportional to the intensity of light received. While the gridded pattern is systematically scanned, the signals are converted to numbers in proportion to their strength, and the numbers, in binary form, are then stored in electromagnetic form. With or without alteration by

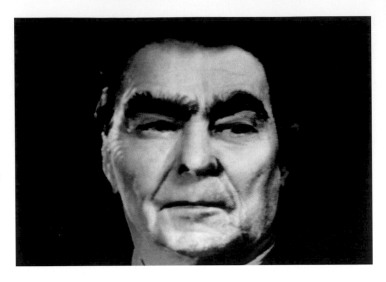

further computer manipulation, the images can be regenerated, via different mechanisms, onto a television screen, or onto photographic prints or film, or onto paper. In each case the stored signals are again laid out in the geometric pattern of the mosaic, but the rectangular reticulation is rarely visible because of the extreme densities of the original grid and replicating mechanisms. The technology for producing a digital image is formidable and in flux.

DIMENSIONS

In stating the measurements of photographs, height is given before width, and dimensions are usually stated metrically and in inches. Normally it is the size of the image itself that is measured rather than the sheet on which it appears.

DIRECT-POSITIVE PRINT

The term *direct positive* can be used to refer to the result of any photographic process in which a positive image is produced on paper, glass, or metal, without a separate negative. Several modern processes fall under this rubric, including those for making slides, transparency films, and DYE DESTRUCTION prints; those for photocopying documents; and those involving reversal materials. A narrower use of the term denotes simpler nineteenth-century processes, most notably that of Hippolyte Bayard (1801–1887). In 1839 and shortly afterward, Bayard produced images by coating a sheet of good quality writing paper with silver chloride, nearly exactly as Talbot had done for PHOTOGENIC DRAWINGS. Unlike Talbot, Bayard then exposed the paper to light until it blackened. After dipping it in potassium iodide, he placed the blotted sheet in a camera, where the iodine bleached out the paper in proportion to the light received, forming a positive image. After learning of Sir John Herschel's idea of using sodium thiosulfate ("hypo") as a fixer, Bayard employed hypo instead of the potassium bromide he had initially used. The print was then washed. Each print was unique and could not be duplicated except by new photography. His direct-positive prints can be yellow-brown to yellowish green in hue, and the image is often so softly rendered as to seem photographed through a gauzy veil or under water.

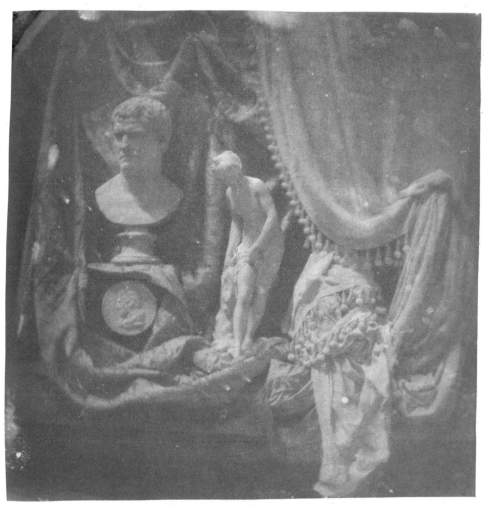

DIRECT-POSITIVE PRINT
Hippolyte Bayard (French, 1801–1887). *Still Life with Statuettes*, 1839.
Direct-positive print, 13.1 × 12.8 cm (5¼ × 5⅟₁₆ in.). JPGM, 84.XM.261.2.

DODGING

When a photographer determines that a dark area of a negative, contact print, or trial proof is too dense or shows inadequate detail, she or he can employ dodging as a technique to reduce that density. During enlargement it consists of interposing for part of the exposure a piece of card, tin, plastic, or aluminum, which is attached to the end of a thin stiff wire between the beam of light coming through the negative via the enlarging lens and the new print being exposed. The shadow cast by the card reduces the exposure on that area of the print, leaving it lighter in tone or showing greater detail. To avoid creating a sharp outline around the shadowed area, the photographer jiggles the dodging instrument gently back and forth. If a photographer uses dodging while contact printing, he or she interposes the card between the light source and the negative. For a related technique, see BURNING-IN.

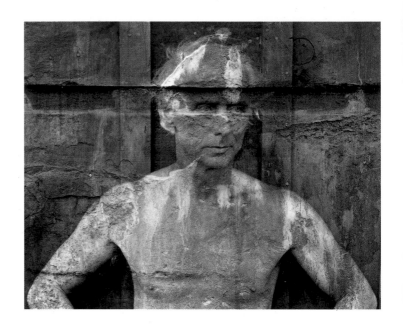

DOUBLE EXPOSURE
Frederick Sommer
(American, 1905)
Max Ernst, 1944
Gelatin silver print
19.3 × 24.1 cm
(7⅝ × 9½ in.)
JPGM
86.XM.515

DOUBLE EXPOSURE

A double exposure results from the (presumably) intentional second exposure in a camera of a negative in order to produce a combination of two images in a single print from that negative. Multiple exposures, also for artistic effect, are likewise possible, particularly with the aid of stroboscopic lighting.

DRY PLATE

In general, dry plate refers to any glass or metal plate coated with a dried light-sensitive emulsion. The first true dry plates were of glass coated with ALBUMEN containing SILVER SALTS. As they were less sensitive and therefore required much longer exposures than WET-COLLODION plates, dry plates were little employed. So-called DRY-COLLODION plates (which were in fact very slightly damp rather than dry) also required longer exposures than wet collodion and were also little used. The term *dry plate* usually refers to thin glass plates coated with gelatin containing light-sensitive silver salts. The first practical plates of this type were invented in 1871 by Richard Maddox (1816–1902) and after a period of rapid evolution were in general use in the mid-1880s; they are still available, although infrequently used. Dry plates wholly supplanted wet collodion as they did not require messy last-minute chemical preparations and were more sensitive. A photographer normally bought the plates already sensitized, in the size for which her or his camera was designed, although in the early days some photographers coated their own.

DRYSTAMP	See BLINDSTAMP.

DYE DESTRUCTION PRINT /DYE BLEACH PROCESS

These color prints are made from a color transparency or negative in which the print material has, at the outset, at least three emulsion layers of SILVER SALTS (halides). Each of the three layers is sensitized to one of the three primary colors of light: blue, green, and red. Thus, each layer can record different information about the color make-up of the image. (The green layer "remembers" green, and so on.) Each layer also contains a dye related to the primary color to which the layer is SENSITIZED. During exposure to the negative, in each layer a silver image is formed. This image is developed and then bleached out, and with it a proportional amount of the associated dye is also destroyed. After additional chemical manipulation, the print is FIXED and WASHED. The residual dyes, on a white support, form a full-color image in which the three emulsion layers are perceived as one. (Cibachrome is one of the trade names for a print made in this way. Cibachromes have a high gloss and, where visible, black margins.) The vibrant color in a dye destruction print is relatively resistant to fading, although not as resistant as the color in a DYE TRANSFER print; however, it is more permanent than a CHROMOGENIC print. (Illustration on next page.)

DYE DIFFUSION PRINT

This type of modern color print is made by a highly sophisticated technology that can only be approximately described here. The emulsion of the print material has three principal layers, each sensitized to one of the three primary colors of light: red, green,

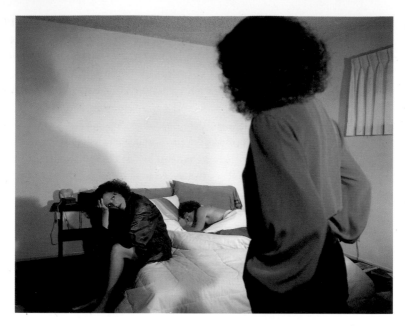

DYE DESTRUCTION PRINT/DYE BLEACH PROCESS
Eileen Cowin (American, b. 1947). *Untitled*, 1981. Dye bleach print (Cibachrome),
47.3×58.8 cm (19×24 in.). Los Angeles County Museum of Art,
Graphic Arts Council Curatorial Discretionary Fund, M.84.17.

DYE DIFFUSION PRINT
William Wegman
(American, b. 1943)
*Ray and Mrs. Lubner
in Bed Watching TV*, 1982
Dye diffusion print
(Polaroid)
50.8×60.9 cm (20×24 in.)
Center for Creative
Photography, Tucson

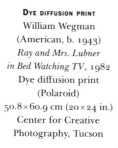

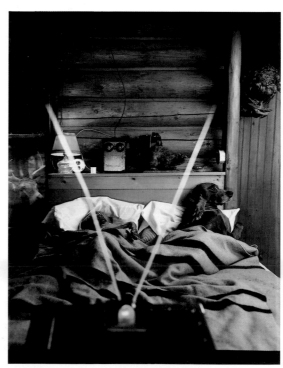

or blue. Each layer is interleaved with an associated layer containing both a dye reciprocal to the primary color and a developing agent. These layers plus a final backing layer comprise both the positive and negative and are contained in a sort of envelope that also holds a pod of additional chemicals. After exposure, the pod breaks open to start the development and dyeing processes. The dyes that form the image diffuse, that is, migrate from their original positions through the emulsion layers to the backing, where they form the final image. The negative materials are then stripped away from this positive, which constitutes a unique color print. The Polaroid process, invented by Edwin Land (1909–1991) and marketed from 1948 onward, is an example of this technology. In a newer version of the process, it is no longer necessary to strip away the negative materials, which remain embedded but not visible in the finished print. Unfortunately, because of unused chemicals remaining in the negative materials, these newer prints are less stable than their predecessors.

DYE TRANSFER PRINT
(DYE IMBIBITION PRINT)

These two terms refer to a class of color prints made by a series of related processes in which three carefully superimposed layers of dye are transferred to a gelatin-coated base. Generally, from a color transparency, three separation negatives in black and white are made by photographing the original negative successively through red, green, and blue filters. Each negative thus carries information about part of the color composition. From each

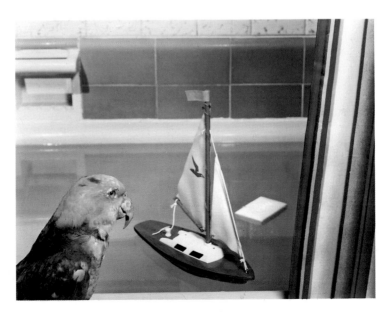

DYE TRANSFER PRINT
(DYE IMBIBITION PRINT)
Jo Ann Callis
(American, b. 1941)
Parrot and Sailboat, 1980
Dye transfer print
45 × 58 cm
(17⅜ × 22¾ in.)
Ralph M. Parsons Fund
Los Angeles County
Museum of Art
M.85.120.6

negative a matrix (or mold) is made by exposing under it a gelatin-coated film and developing this film in a solution that contains a tanner which hardens the part of the gelatin that has been exposed. The balance of the gelatin is washed away, leaving a mold. Each of the three molds is placed in a different dye bath, appropriate to the color of the filter by which its separation negative was made. The molds are then serially applied in exact alignment to gelatin-coated paper to which the three dyes are transferred, thus producing a full-color image. The dye transfer process, which has considerably evolved from its origins in the 1870s, is time-consuming but permits considerable control of results and produces a relatively permanent print that does not contain silver. For a related earlier process, see CARBRO print.

EDITION

An edition is created when a photographer decides for commercial purposes to set a maximum number of prints from a negative and indicates the limitation by serially marking each print with two numbers in the form of a fraction. The numerator denotes the position of the print in the sequence, presumably in the order actually made, and the denominator the total number of prints. This practice is borrowed from traditional printmaking processes.

EMULSION

The light-sensitive coating of modern photographic film, plates, and printing paper is an emulsion consisting of silver-halide crystals suspended in gelatin. (An emulsion consists of tiny undissolved particles of one substance held in suspension, in uniform dispersion, in another substance, initially liquid or semi-liquid in form, as, for example, mayonnaise consists of particles of egg yolk held in oil.) The light-sensitive silver halides, or SILVER SALTS, are silver bromide, silver chloride, and silver iodide. The properties of these halides are varied, and other ingredients are added, depending on the particular use for which the emulsion is designed. After manufacture, the emulsion is applied to a final support, transparent if for film, opaque if for prints. (See GELATIN SILVER print.) In the nineteenth century, ALBUMEN and COLLODION were the primary means of attaching silver-halide crystals to supports, but the halides rested on the surfaces of these substances and were not suspended within them.

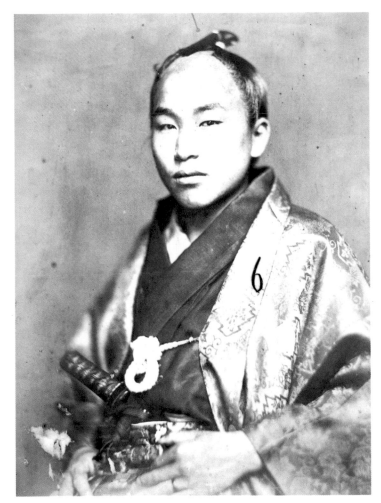

ENLARGEMENT
Alexander Gardner
(American, b. Scotland,
1821–1882)
and Mathew Brady
(American, c. 1823–1896)
Tateisi Owasjere, Interpreter
for the Japanese Delegation
1860
Solar enlarged albumen
print from a
wet-collodion-on-glass
negative, showing loss of
detail.
38.2 × 31.7 cm
(15⅛ × 12½ in.)
JPGM
84.XM.479.33

ENLARGEMENT

An enlargement is a photographic print of greater dimensions than the negative from which it was made. (A print of the same size as the negative is called a CONTACT print.) The overall process for making an enlargement is to concentrate a source of light, usually by means of a lens, sending the light first through a negative and then through a second, magnifying lens, onto light-sensitive paper of the desired size. The quality of the enlargement is thus dependent on the enlarging apparatus, the degree of transparency of the negative, and the degree of sensitivity to light of the material used to produce the final print. In the nineteenth century, exposures were long, as the usual source of light was the sun; in the twentieth century, electric light has resulted in much shorter exposures. Enlargement can also be used to make an enlarged transparency from which, in turn, a contact negative

45

and then a single print or series of same-size prints can be produced. Enlargements became truly practicable with the advent of emulsions containing silver bromide, which were sensitive even to artificial light, such as gaslight in the 1880s.

The great advantages of enlarging negatives are twofold: to increase the scale of the finished print and to shrink the size of the camera used to produce them, making unnecessary the cumbersome cameras of the glass-plate era, when enlarging often had unpredictable results.

EXPOSURE   See APERTURE.

FERROTYPE   See TINTYPE.

FIELD CAMERA   See VIEW CAMERA.

FIXING   Fixing is a critical step in the production of a photograph. At the end of the development of a negative or a print the chemical compounds on the surface of either, which compose the image, are unstable and therefore need to be treated by fixing to prevent further chemical reactions. After development and preliminary washing, negatives or prints are immersed in one or more baths containing a fixer and, usually, other compounds to abet the process and strengthen the results. Careful timing and control of chemical purities are required. Further washing follows. Sir John Herschel first suggested in 1839 that sodium hyposulfite could be used to fix photographs. Although the correct name for the compound is sodium thiosulfate, it was for so long the most common fixer that photographers today tend to call all fixers "hypo," even though other chemicals are often used.

FLASH   A photographic flash is the addition, for an instant or two, of supplemental light of high intensity to a photographic subject in order to produce a better-exposed negative and thus a more visible final image. Perhaps the earliest device for this purpose was the magnesium-flare used in the early 1860s. Modern devices include the flashbulb and the electronic flash.

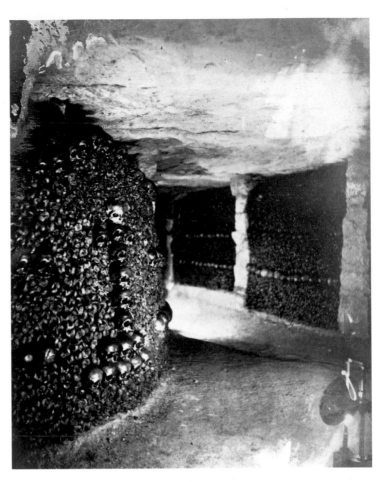

FLASH
Nadar
(Gaspard-Félix
Tournachon)
(French, 1820–1910)
Paris Catacombs, 1865
Albumen print
22.5 × 18.2 cm
(3 × 1¾in.)
JPGM
84.XM.436.481
with detail showing
magnesium lamp

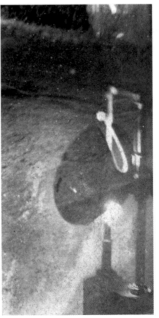

FOXING

This term refers to brownish spots in paper. They are caused by fungus, bacteria, and/or chemical or metallic impurities introduced in the paper-manufacturing process, which, when exposed to atmospheric moisture over time, cause staining in the paper and sometimes thereby on a photograph made on or mounted to that paper.

GELATIN SILVER PRINT /SILVER-BROMIDE PRINT /SILVER-CHLORIDE PRINT

Soon after the invention of the gelatin DRY PLATE in 1871, papers coated with gelatin containing SILVER SALTS for making black-and-white prints from negatives were introduced, and they are still in general use. The silver salts contained in the gelatin emulsion laid on the paper are principally silver bromide or silver chloride or a combination of both. As silver chloride is less sensitive to light than silver bromide, papers containing silver chloride are used for CONTACT PRINTING, whereas silver bromide papers are primarily used for ENLARGEMENTS. Papers with both salts—chloro-bromide papers—can be used for either method of making prints.

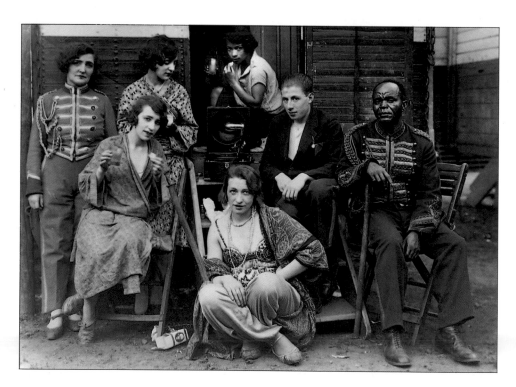

GELATIN SILVER PRINT
August Sander (German, 1876–1964). *Group of Circus People*, 1926.
Gelatin silver print, 19.9×27.5 cm (7¹³⁄₁₆×10⅞ in.). JPGM, 84.XM.498.5.

In 1873 gelatin silver-bromide papers were invented and first produced by Peter Mawdsley, although they did not come into general use until the 1880s. They were DEVELOPING-OUT papers rather than PRINTING-OUT papers, that is, after brief exposure under a negative, usually in an enlarger, the image was further brought out by chemical development. Gelatin silver-chloride papers for printing-out and for developing-out were both introduced in 1882. A printed-out photograph was placed under the negative under a light source until the image appeared in its final form, without chemical development. The exposure under the negative was necessarily much longer than for a developed-out photograph. Photographers of the 1880s and afterward did not normally coat their own papers but obtained them from commercial sources. Gelatin silver prints had generally displaced ALBUMEN prints in popularity by 1895 because they were more stable, did not yellow, and were simpler and quicker to produce.

Because of the great variety of papers offered by manufacturers, the tones and surface gloss of gelatin silver prints varied. Generally, however, the tone of the image of a gelatin silver-bromide print is neutral black. A gelatin silver-chloride print that has been developed out is bluish black or cool in tone, while one that has been printed out (a comparative rarity in America after 1895) is brown or warm in tone. Prints made on paper containing both bromide and chloride have a warm, brownish black tone. All of these colors can be altered by TONING. The highlights are white unless the underlying paper support has been TINTED. Gelatin silver prints often, but not always, have high surface gloss, particularly if they are contact prints.

GHOST

During the long exposures required by nineteenth-century photographic processes, if a person, animal, or carriage moved away from its initial position, a blurred, faint, residual impression of it remained on the negative and appeared in the print. This image is called a ghost from its transparent, whitish tone. Any exposure of a negative with a shutter speed slower than about $\frac{1}{60}$ of a second can cause objects in motion to blur. Sometimes this fact was used to intentionally produce a ghostlike image. See also SPIRIT PHOTOGRAPH. (Illustration on next page.)

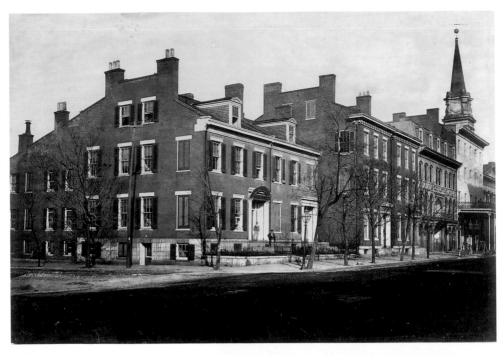

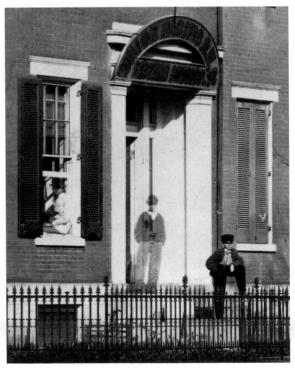

GHOST
Alexander Gardner
(American, b. Scotland,
1821–1882)
*St. Louis Office,
Union Pacific Railroad*
1867
Albumen print
33.3 × 47.5 cm
(12¾ × 18¹¹⁄₁₆ in.)
JPGM, 84.XM.1027.8
with enlarged detail
showing ghost

GLASS PLATE / MAMMOTH PLATE

In 1834, Sir John Herschel presciently suggested that glass, because of its transparency, could be employed as a support for light-sensitive materials. From 1850 onward, glass was used for positives, like the AMBROTYPE, or, more frequently, for photographic negatives. ALBUMEN, COLLODION, and GELATIN, carrying light-sensitive SILVER SALTS, have all been successfully employed for coating glass plates for use in the camera. Glass has also been used for transparencies like the LANTERN SLIDE. The term *glass plate* most often applies to the collodion process. Plates of high-quality glass with ground edges were commercially available in standard sizes. Mammoth plates are simply those plates of large dimensions (and considerable weight), typically 18 by 22 inches (46 by 56 cm), often used for photographing landscapes during the nineteenth century. In the twentieth century, glass plates can be taken to refer to dry plates carrying gelatin emulsions.

GROUND GLASS

In modern usage the term *ground glass* denotes the translucent surface in a camera on which the subject of a photograph is projected from the lens via a mirror and prism to show the same image that will be exposed on the negative. The photographer uses it to assess, compose, and focus the image.

GUM BICHROMATE PRINT

Introduced in 1894, popular into the 1920s, and occasionally used today, the gum bichromate process for making prints from negatives was valued for the high degree of artistic control it gave the photographer over the appearance of the final print. A gum bichromate print was made by brushing onto a sheet of paper a smooth coating of gum arabic (a transparent plant secretion) dissolved in water and mixed with a pigment and a solution of potassium (or ammonium) bichromate. The coated paper was dried and exposed in sunlight or ultraviolet light under a same-size negative, i.e., was CONTACT PRINTED. The bichromate caused the gum arabic to harden in proportion to the amount of light received. For example, in what would be the highlights of the final print, the negative was dark. As a result, over the corresponding section of the print the gum did not harden and could be washed away, leaving the highlight area light in tone. After exposure, the print was placed in water, and the part of the gum that had remained soluble slowly dissolved amd floated away. The photographer could alter this process by brushing the surface or focusing a stream of water toward it to dissolve greater or lesser amounts of the pigmented gum arabic, thus changing the degrees of contrast. The print was complete when dried.

The print, however, was often recoated with the same or a pigmented gum-arabic solution of another color. It was then re-exposed once it had been carefully aligned under the same negative in order to alter, deepen, or enrich its tones, overall or in specific areas. Gum bichromate prints have broad tones with little resolution of detail, and they often resemble crayon or charcoal drawings or watercolors. As they do not contain silver in the final image, they are relatively permanent.

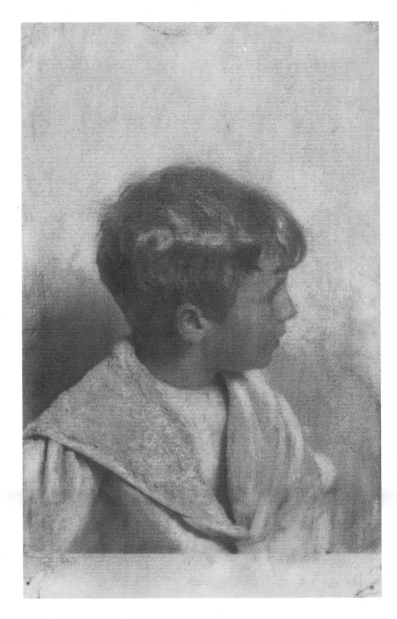

GUM BICHROMATE PRINT
Robert Demachy
(French, 1859–1936)
Jack Demachy, Age Eight
1904
Gum bichromate print
15.9 × 11.2 cm
(6¼ × 4⁷⁄₁₆ in.)
JPGM
84.XM.806.5

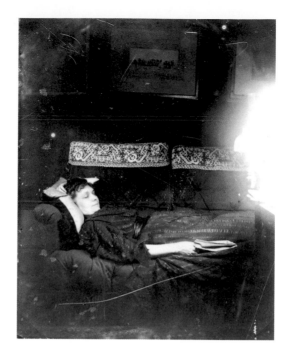

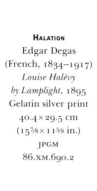
HALATION

This technical term refers to a halo of light around a bright object in a photograph, such as a window, lamp, or streetlight. It occurs in the negative or in the positive printing process because of excess light rays from the brilliant object reflecting back from the emulsion support, whether glass or film. Antihalation coatings exist to eliminate such reflections.

HALFTONE

The halftone processes refer to the transformation of the continuous tones of a photographic image, from the whites through the grays (halftones) to the blacks, into the discontinuous tones of a printed image. To create grays from a single tone of black printing ink, the ink can either be deposited in varying densities (as in the photoengraving processes) or in varying patterns of distribution over the page surface (as in the PHOTOLITHOGRAPHIC processes). Halftone usually refers to the photolithographic processes in which the original photographic image is rephotographed through a gridded screen that breaks up the image into a pattern of dots of various sizes, depending on the relative darkness of the original. (These dots are so small that the eye does not see them as dots but as varying shades of gray.) This new image, which has been, in effect, filtered through the screen, can then be transferred to a printing plate.

In the photoengraving processes the continuous tones are

broken into discontinuous tones by dusting the printing plate with powdered resin (called a grain) that diffuses the image. This is similar to the grain used in the traditional aquatint printmaking process. The only photomechanical process that used neither a screen nor a grain was the WOODBURYTYPE.

Both photolithography and photoengraving have numerous technological variations but have largely been superseded by electronic means of producing images from photographs, often involving the use of linear scanners, photo cells, lasers, and the like.

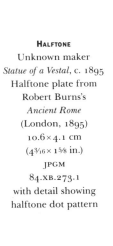

HALFTONE
Unknown maker
Statue of a Vestal, c. 1895
Halftone plate from
Robert Burns's
Ancient Rome
(London, 1895)
10.6 × 4.1 cm
(4 3/16 × 1 5/8 in.)
JPGM
84.XB.273.1
with detail showing
halftone dot pattern

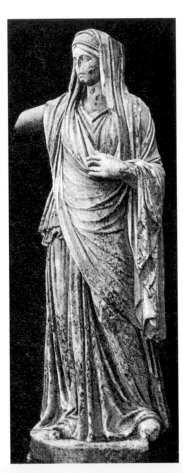

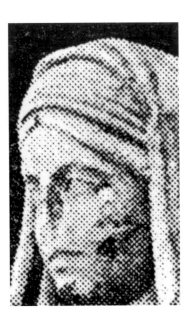

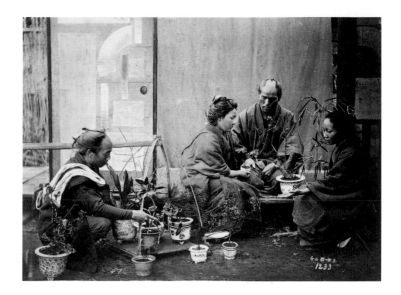

HAND-COLORED PHOTOGRAPH

A variety of means have been used since the days of the DAGUERREO-TYPE to add color manually to the surface of black-and-white photographs, including watercolor and other paints and dyes. Brushes, cotton swabs, and airbrushes are used for application. Hand-colored photographs are to be distinguished from TINTED ones.

HELIOGRAVURE

See PHOTOGRAVURE.

HOLOGRAM

A hologram is an image in three dimensions made on a photographic plate, but it is not, in this writer's view, a photograph. Although holograms and photographs share the quality of being images and the characteristic of being made by the exposure of an emulsion surface to light directed by lenses, in all other respects they differ.

The technology and vocabulary for holography are complex, and several kinds of images are called holograms; what follows is a simplified sketch. One kind of hologram, a transmission hologram, is made by directing one of two parts of a laser-generated beam of light toward an emulsion on a glass plate. The other part of the beam is directed toward the subject of the hologram and reflected from the subject toward the emulsion. The coincidence of the two beams of light on the emulsion produces a mixture of the patterns each provides. The emulsion records the similarities and differences of light. (This is a little as if yellow and blue paint were mixed on a surface to produce green, but at each point on the surface the differences between yellow and blue as well as the resultant green were apparent.) If the finished glass plate is illuminated, again using a laser, an image that appears to have three dimensions is produced in a space set up to receive it. A reflection hologram is made somewhat differently and can be viewed by reflected light without projection. Its image is contained in the many thin layers of which it is made. Reflection holograms are often to be found on present-day credit cards and the like.

"Hypo"   See FIXING.

Inscription   Anything written or otherwise marked on the front (recto) or back (verso) of a photograph, its mount, or, less frequently, its mat, is an inscription. Inscriptions can consist of the photographer's signature or BLIND- or WETSTAMP, or they can be made by someone else entirely, for example, a dedication of the photograph by one friend to another. (See also the illustration accompanying LANTERN SLIDE.)

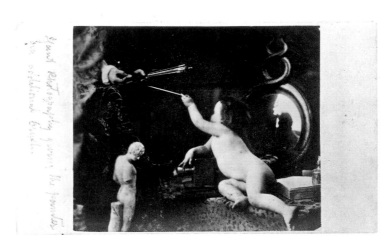

INSCRIPTION
Oscar Gustave Rejlander
(British, b. Sweden,
1813–1875)
*The Infant Photography
Giving the Painter
an Additional Brush*
c. 1856
Albumen print
with inscribed title
60 × 71 cm
(2⅜ × 2¹³/₁₆ in.)
JPGM
84.XP.458.34

Kallitype   The kallitype is an iron-salt photographic process devised about
/van dyke print   1899 by W. J. Nichol and derived from the work of Sir John Herschel in the 1840s. The process is analogous to that for the PLATINUM print, and the results can look similar. A thick stock of paper was brushed with a solution of ferric oxalate (which is an iron salt), oxalic acid, and silver nitrate. This light-sensitive paper was CONTACT PRINTED under a negative, usually in sunlight, until the midtones began to appear. The print was then developed out in one of several solutions, depending on the color desired.

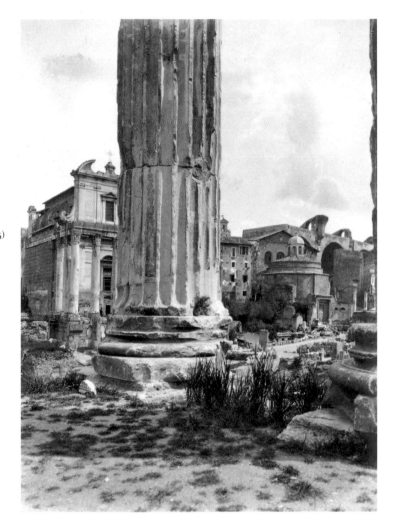

The light had transformed the ferric oxalate to ferrous oxalate
and produced an image in metallic silver. The print was then
FIXED with sodium thiosulfate and WASHED. Its color, which could
be further modified by TONING, could be black, brown, sepia,
purple, or maroon. Because of the kallitype's alleged imperma-
nence—Nichol's original formula for fixing was deficient—it
never achieved real popularity, although many variants of the
process were announced. One kind of kallitype was known as a
Van Dyke print, as its rich, deep browns are thought to resemble
those achieved by Anthony van Dyck, or those of the pigment
named after him.

Lantern slide

In the mid-nineteenth century, when a slide projector was popularly called a magic lantern, a lantern slide was the source of the projected image. Originally an image painted on glass, a lantern slide became photographic in the 1850s with the use of an ALBUMEN, or later COLLODION, coating on one side. Either kind of coating contained light-sensitive SILVER SALTS, which, when exposed under a negative, DEVELOPED, FIXED, and WASHED, produced a positive transparency. To protect the fragile finished image, the coated side was covered with a second, same-sized piece of glass (usually about 3¼ by 3¼ inches [8.2 by 8.2 cm]), and their edges were taped together. Lantern slides were used both for home entertainment and for the illustration of public lectures, often of an edifying nature.

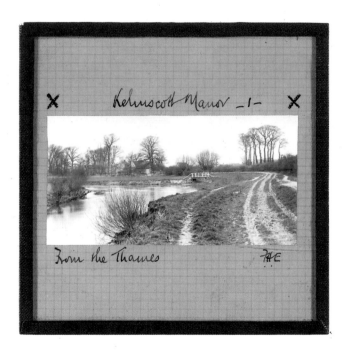

LANTERN SLIDE
Frederick Evans
(British, 1853–1943)
Kelmscott Manor,
from the Thames, c. 1896
Lantern slide
Image:
3.5 × 6.7 cm
(1⅜ × 2⅝ in.)
JPGM
84.XH.1616.33

Lens

Made of glass or plastic, a lens is the essential means by which light rays coming from an object being photographed are directed onto the negative material in a camera in order to produce a photograph. Light rays travel in straight lines, but when they pass from one medium (in this case, air) to another (in this case, the glass of a lens), they bend. They bend again as they emerge from the back of the lens. The front and back surface contours of a lens determine the direction in which the rays are bent. Camera lenses are shaped so that the light rays converge on the negative. Modern camera lenses are not single pieces of glass but assemblies of multiple glass elements that collectively produce a clear, distortion-free image. The quality of a lens depends upon the precision of its design and manufacture. Among the many kinds manufactured for specific purposes are wide-angle, telephoto, soft-focus, enlarging, and zoom lenses.

MAMMOTH PLATE   See GLASS PLATE.

MAT   See MOUNT.

MINIATURE CAMERA   This inexact term designates a very easily portable camera meant to be hand-held, having a lens of a high standard of sharpness, employing roll film (particularly 35mm), and thus producing a small negative that requires considerable enlargement. The term is used particularly for cameras of the Leica type introduced in 1925 by Ernst Leitz (1871–1956); it does not refer to tiny novelty cameras.

MONTAGE   See COLLAGE.

MOUNT/MAT   In American parlance a mount is a secondary support to which a photograph is affixed, the primary support being the paper on which the photograph itself was made. A mount is normally cut from heavy paper stock or card, preferably of good quality and acid-free. If a second sheet with an opening cut into it of the size and proportion of the photograph is hinged to the mount, the ensemble is called a mat. The top sheet through the window of which the image is seen is called an overmat in America, a passe-partout in England, where *mat* and *mount* are more nearly synonymous terms. For safe handling, a photograph should have both mount and mat.

To attach a photograph to its mount, modern conservators prefer to use thin hinges, like those used to put stamps in albums but made of rice paper, affixed to an edge of the photograph with wheat-starch paste.

NEGATIVE/POSITIVE   As William Henry Fox Talbot discovered in the mid-1830s, when a sheet of paper carrying light-sensitive SILVER SALTS is exposed to light, the silver darkens in proportion to the amount of light reflected from the subject. An image of the scene outside the camera is formed on the surface of the paper, but where an object in the actual scene is light in value, its appearance on the paper is dark and where dark, light. It was Talbot's genius to realize that

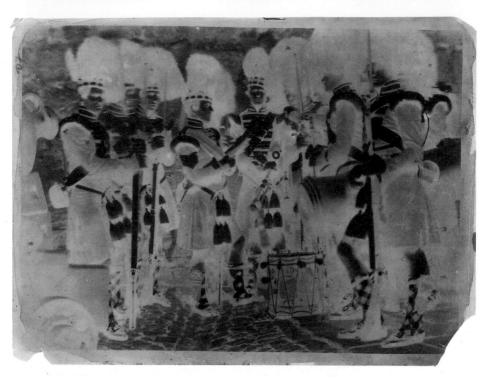

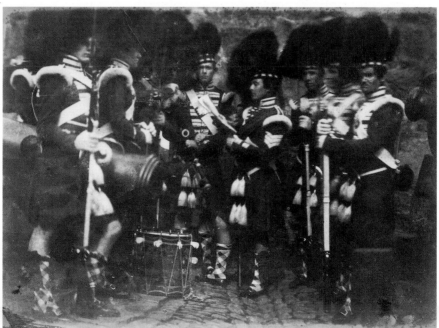

NEGATIVE/POSITIVE

David Octavius Hill (British, 1802–1870) and Robert Adamson (British, 1821–1848). *Sergeant of the Forty-second Gordon Highlanders Reading the Orders of the Day*, 1846.
Calotype (negative) and salt print (positive), each 14.5 × 16.7 cm (5¾ × 7¾ in.).
JPGM, 84.XM.445.18 and 84.XM.445.3.

if this piece of paper, the negative, were placed in contact with a second sheet of similarly sensitized paper, the values on the second sheet would be returned to normal by reversal, that is, would correspond to the actual values. The second sheet is a positive, commonly called a print. The names *negative* and *positive* were suggested by Sir John Herschel. Talbot also realized that multiple positives could be made from a single negative. From this negative-positive process, all subsequent photography derives.

NEGATIVE PRINT

In this kind of print, the highlights and shadows are the reverse of their normal appearance: the shadows are light, the highlights are dark. Negative prints, made for artistic effect, can be achieved by a number of means, including placing photographic paper normally used for prints in the camera in lieu of film, photographing a negative, or printing from a positive transparency.

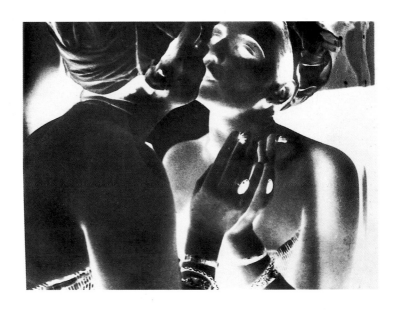

NEGATIVE PRINT
Franz Roh
(German, 1890–1965)
Selbstbegrussung, c. 1930
Gelatin silver print
15.4 × 19.8 cm
(6 ¹⁄₁₆ × 7 ¹³⁄₁₆ in.)
JPGM
84.XP.260.133

OIL-PIGMENT PRINT

See BROMOIL PRINT.

OROTONE

This term refers to a photographic image made from a negative that had been printed on a glass plate covered with a GELATIN SILVER emulsion. The back of the glass plate was then painted with gold mixed with banana oil or with bronze powders mixed in resin to give the appearance of gold, and the work was framed. The technique was popularized by Edward Sheriff Curtis (1868–1952).

ORTHOCHROMATIC /PANCHROMATIC

These descriptive terms apply to photographic negative materials that have been adjusted to produce fuller ranges of response to the color spectrum. The light-sensitive SILVER SALTS that form photographic images respond more strongly to blue light than to the balance of the spectrum, while the human eye responds most to green light. Thus, the black-and-white tonal values of mid-nineteenth-century photographs, particularly of works of art, did not correspond to actuality. Red and yellow areas appeared too dark, blues and violets too light. To correct these deficiencies, at a later period dyes were added to emulsions to enhance their color sensitivity. From the early 1880s, an orthochromatic (correct color) emulsion sensitive to blue and green light, but not red light, was available. After 1905, a panchromatic (all color) emulsion, sensitive to blue, green, and, to a lesser extent, red light, was produced. Further refinements followed.

**PALLADIOTYPE
(PALLADIUM PRINT)**

See PLATINUM PRINT.

PANORAMA

A panorama consists of a photograph or series of photographs that encompasses a sweeping view. When an ordinary camera and lens are used to produce a panorama, the camera is carefully pivoted on a tripod and a series of exposures of slightly overlapping aspects of the same view are made. The resultant segments are then trimmed and pieced together. Wide-angle lenses or panoramic cameras can produce single-exposure panoramas. From the daguerrean era onward, many varieties of panoramic cameras have been invented. In one kind of modern camera, the film is mounted on a curved back inside the camera and the lens automatically turns on an axis. A continuous exposure is made onto the film through a narrow slit moving with the lens. Another camera itself rotates, and the film moves past a slit at a speed coordinated to that of the rotation. A camera called a cyclograph was devised to photograph in a continuous band around the outside of a cylindrical object. In this instance, the object rather than the camera was made to revolve, but exposure was again through a slit.

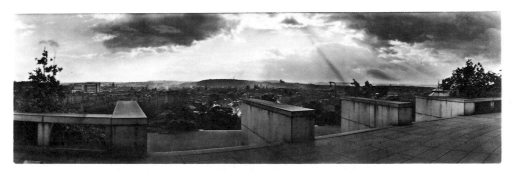

PANORAMA
Josef Sudek (Czechoslovak, 1896–1976). *Panorama of Prague*, c. 1946.
Gelatin silver print, 15.9×50.7 cm (6¼×20 in.). JPGM, 86.XM.516.1.

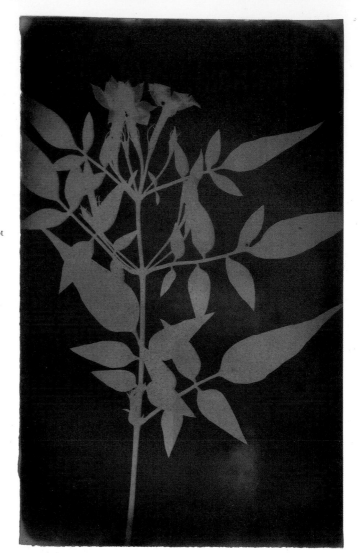

PHOTOGENIC DRAWING

Photogenic drawing was William Henry Fox Talbot's name for the
results of his first, cameraless photographic process and derived
from experiments he had begun in 1834 but did not announce
until 1839. In its simplest form the process required a smooth,
high-quality sheet of writing paper that was dried after immersion
in a solution of table salt (sodium chloride). Talbot then brushed
the paper with a solution of silver nitrate that combined with
the sodium chloride to produce silver chloride, which is a light-
sensitive SILVER SALT. In sunlight on top of this sheet of sensitized
paper Talbot then placed small objects such as leaves and lace. Those
areas of the paper where the sunlight fell darkened, while those

areas that the object prevented sunlight from reaching remained light. The exposure continued until the image (in negative) was completely PRINTED OUT and thus wholly visible. Talbot prevented the paper from continuing to darken, i.e., he FIXED the image, however imperfectly, with a strong solution of ordinary salt that rendered the unexposed silver salt less light-sensitive.

Talbot's next step was to expose sensitized paper inside simple cameras of his own design: small wooden boxes with a lens at the end opposite the paper. The results were the first, rudimentary camera negatives. Talbot placed these negative images in sunlight on top of and in contact with a second sheet of sensitized paper until a completely formed image had printed out on the second sheet. This was a positive print, the lights and darks now corresponding to those seen by the eye. These prints were similarly fixed by means of a strong table-salt solution or, later, potassium bromide or iodide.

As photogenic drawings were highly experimental and often only partially fixed (and thus subject to fading), their appearance varies considerably from reddish tones to the palest lemons and lilacs, depending on which chemicals Talbot used.

PHOTOGLYPHIC ENGRAVING

Photoglyphic engraving, William Henry Fox Talbot's improved process for producing a printing plate from a photograph, was patented in 1858. It depends on the principle that gelatin sensitized with potassium bichromate is rendered insoluble

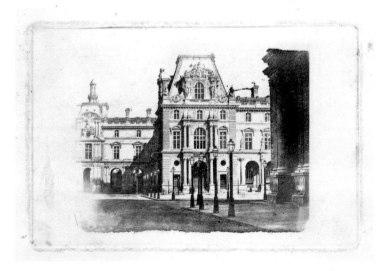

PHOTOGLYPHIC ENGRAVING
William Henry Fox Talbot
(British, 1800–1877)
The New Louvre, Paris
1858
Photoglyphic engraving
from a negative
attributed to
A. Clouzard (French,
active 1854–1859)
and Charles Soulier
(French, 1840–1875)
5.5 × 7 cm
(2⅛ × 2¾ in.)
JPGM
84.XM.478.13

by exposure to light in proportion to the amount of light received. After coating a copper plate with bichromated gelatin, Talbot exposed the plate to light under a positive transparency of the image he wished to reproduce. It was then dusted with powdered resin and heated to evenly distribute the resinous particles. The plate was etched in an acid solution that simultaneously dissolved away the part of the gelatin that had not hardened and bit away those same areas. After cleaning, the plate was inked and the surface wiped clean, ink remaining in the etched cavities. Under pressure, it was printed on paper, thus creating a reproduction of the original image. (The resin dusting functioned much as it did in the traditional aquatint printmaking process by breaking continuous tones into discontinuous tones; see HALFTONE.) Talbot sometimes also employed a gauze screen to the same end. He coined the term *photoglyph* from the Greek for *carved light*.

PHOTOGLYPTIE   See WOODBURYTYPE.

PHOTOGRAM   A photogram is a kind of photograph, although made without a camera or lens by placing an object or objects on top of a piece of

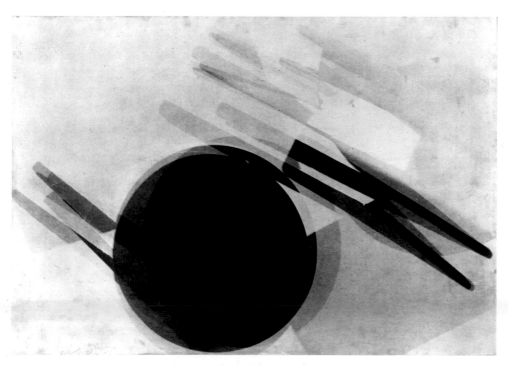

PHOTOGRAM
László Moholy-Nagy (American, b. Hungary, 1895–1946). *Photogram Number 1: The Mirror*, 1922/23.
Gelatin silver photogram, 63.8×92.1 cm (25⅛×36¼ in.). JPGM, 84.XM.450.1.

paper or film coated with light-sensitive materials and then exposing the paper or film to light. Where the object covers the paper, the paper remains unexposed and light in tone; where it does not cover, the paper darkens. If the object is translucent, midtones appear. After exposure, the paper is DEVELOPED and FIXED. Among the first photograms were the PHOTOGENIC DRAWINGS produced in the late 1830s by William Henry Fox Talbot, in which some of the objects were ferns, flowers, and pieces of lace. Other examples of photograms were made about 1918 by Christian Schad (1894–1982), who called his works Schadographs; during the 1920s and afterward by Man Ray (1890–1976), who called his photograms Rayographs; and from the 1930s onward by Lázsló Moholy-Nagy (1895–1946).

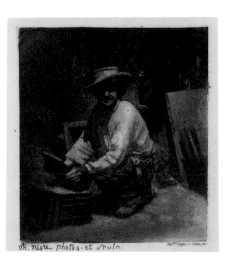

PHOTOGRAVURE
Charles Nègre
(French, 1820–1880)
Kneeling Mason, 1854
Photogravure
5.7 × 5 cm
(2 ¼ × 1 ¹⁵/₁₆ in.)
JPGM
84.XP.453.12

PHOTOGRAVURE

(HELIOGRAVURE)

Photogravure, also known as heliogravure, is (arguably) the finest photomechanical means for reproducing a photograph in large editions. Although descended from the traditional printmaking process of etching and derived from Talbot's PHOTOGLYPHIC ENGRAVING, photogravure was devised by the Austrian printer Karel Klič (1841–1926) in 1879 and further developed by him. It depends on the principle that bichromated gelatin hardens in proportion to its exposure to light. A tissue coated on one side with gelatin sensitized with potassium bichromate was exposed to light under a transparent positive that had been CONTACT PRINTED from the negative of the image to be reproduced. When wet, this tissue was firmly pressed, gelatin side down, onto a copper printing plate that had been prepared with a thin, even dusting of resinous powder. In warm water, the tissue-paper backing was peeled away and those areas of the gelatin that had not been exposed to light dissolved. The copper plate with its remaining unevenly distributed gelatin coating was then placed in an acid bath. Where the gelatin remained thick (the highlights of the print to come), the acid ate away the metal slowly; where the gelatin was thin or absent, the acid bit faster. The plate was thus etched to different depths corresponding to the tones of the original image. When inked, the varying depths held differing amounts of ink. The inked plate was then used in a printing press. From photogravure, Karel Klič developed modern screen gravure (rotogravure), which was widely used in newspaper illustration until its replacement by offset lithography in the 1910s. If untrimmed, a finished photogravure shows the mark of the plate around the image. Its blacks often seem like charcoal and its whites, if printed on high-quality white paper, stay white.

PHOTOLITHOGRAPHY

Photolithography—a process for printing a photographic image—depends like its antecedent the printmaking process of lithography on the principle that grease and water repel each other. Developed in 1855 by Alphonse Louis Poitevin (1819–1882), the photolithographic process begins when a flat stone (*lithos* in Greek) or a metal plate of zinc or aluminum is coated with gelatin (originally ALBUMEN) that has been sensitized with potassium bichromate. When exposed to light under a photographic negative,

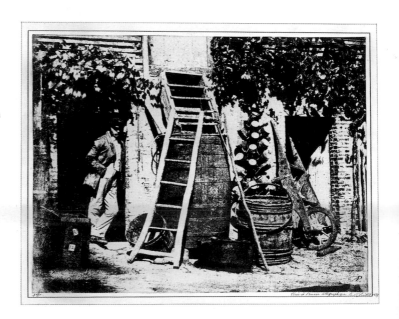

PHOTOLITHOGRAPHY
Alphonse Louis Poitevin
(French, 1819–1882)
*Man with Garden
Implements*, 1855
Photolithograph
20.8 × 27.1 cm
(8³⁄₁₆ × 10¹¹⁄₁₆ in.)
JPGM
84.XP.259.5

the bichromated gelatin is rendered insoluble to water in proportion to the light received. The soluble portions of the gelatin are cleaned from the limestone, which is then dampened and inked. The greasy printer's ink adheres to the areas of hardened gelatin (the darks in the finished image) but is repulsed by the areas of moist stone that do not have a hardened gelatin coating. The stone is then pressed against paper to which the ink is transferred, producing a reproduction of the original image. The delicate and flat finished photolithograph may show the impress of the stone, but no platemark is visible.

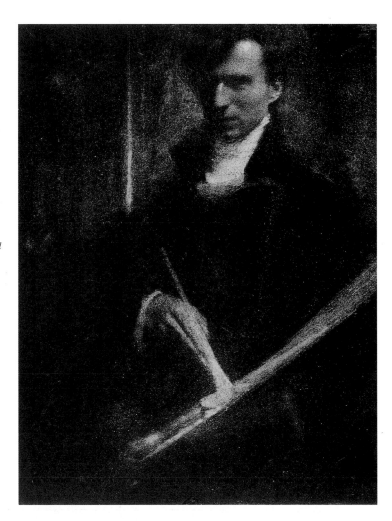

PIGMENT PROCESSES   Pigment processes are any of the various processes that evolved from the 1850s onward in which the final image of the paper is rendered in pigment rather than in the metals silver, iron, platinum, or palladium. They include the BROMOIL, CARBON, CARBRO, and GUM BICHROMATE processes. All depend on the principle that a colloid, such as gum arabic or gelatin, which has been made sensitive to light by the addition of potassium bichromate or the like, hardens on exposure to light in proportion to the amount of light received and so becomes insoluble in water. The pigment processes were popular because of their permanency, their range of possible coloration, their resemblance to traditional artistic media like etching, crayon, charcoal drawing, and watercolor, and the way they could be altered by handwork on their surfaces.

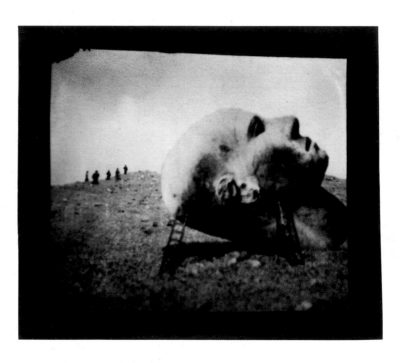

PINHOLE CAMERA

The most elemental form of camera capable of producing a permanent image, the pinhole camera consists of a closed light-proof box with a pinhole opening on one surface. Through the pinhole, light projects an inverted image of the subject onto a flat, light-sensitive material that has been placed on an internal surface opposite the opening. (It is, thus, a miniaturized CAMERA OBSCURA.) As little light enters through the minuscule opening, the negative material must be exposed for a long time. The subjects of prints made from pinhole camera negatives, not having been focused through a lens, have soft overall definition rather than crisp detail.

PLATE:
FULL, HALF, QUARTER,
SIXTH

During the 1840s and later, silver-plated copper plates were commercially produced for making DAGUERREOTYPES. The largest size ordinarily available, from which the others were derived, was the full plate, measuring 6½ by 8½ inches (16.5 by 21.6 cm). Next was the half plate, 4¼ by 5½ inches (10.8 by 13.8 cm). The most common size, the quarter plate, was 3¼ by 4¼ inches (8.3 by 10.8 cm), and the sixth plate, sometimes called the medium plate, was 2¾ by 3¼ inches (7 by 8.3 cm). Ninth and sixteenth plates were less frequently used. When glass plates for negative materials came into use, a parallel nomenclature developed in which 8 by 10 inches (20.3 by 25.4 cm) designated a full plate and 4 by 5 inches (10.2 by 12.7 cm) a quarter plate.

PLATINUM PRINT
/PLATINOTYPE
/PALLADIUM PRINT
/PALLADIOTYPE

The process for making platinum prints was invented in 1873 by William Willis (1841–1923), who continually refined it until 1878, when commercially prepared platinum papers became available through a company he founded. The process depends on the light sensitivity of iron salts. A dried sheet of paper, sensitized with a solution of potassium chloro-platinate and ferric oxalate, an iron salt, was CONTACT PRINTED under a negative in daylight (or another source of strong ultraviolet light) until a faint image was produced by the reaction of the light with the iron salt. The paper was developed by immersion in a solution of potassium oxalate that dissolved out the iron salts and reduced the chloro-platinate salt to platinum in those areas where the exposed iron salts had been. An image in platinum metal replaced one in iron. The paper was washed in a series of weak hydrochloric or citric acid baths to remove remaining excess iron salts and yellow stains formed in the earlier steps. Finally, the print was washed in water.

A variant means of development involved coating the print with differing thicknesses of glycerin, which retarded the action of the developer, potassium oxalate, which was then brushed on. Selective development followed in proportion to the glycerin thickness, producing varieties of intensity and tone. Yet other toning agents were mercuric chloride and lead acetate. Platinum prints were also altered in tone by changing the temperature or composition of the developer or, after development, by immersing the print in solutions containing either uranium nitrate or gold chloride. Olive greens, reds, and blues were all possible, although grays were more usual.

Platinum prints were popular until the 1920s, when the price of platinum rose so steeply as to make them prohibitively expensive. They were in part replaced by the somewhat cheaper palladium prints, the process for which was very nearly the same but which employed a compound of the metal palladium rather than platinum. Both processes were valued for their great range of subtle tonal variations, usually silvery grays, and their permanence. Both have the texture of whatever paper was used. Recently, platinum prints have enjoyed a modest revival.

PLATINUM PRINT
Edward Weston
(American, 1886–1958)
Armco Steel, Armco,
Pipes and Stacks, 1922
Platinum print
24.3 × 19.4 cm
(9⁹⁄₁₆ × 7⅝ in.)
JPGM
86.XM.710.7.

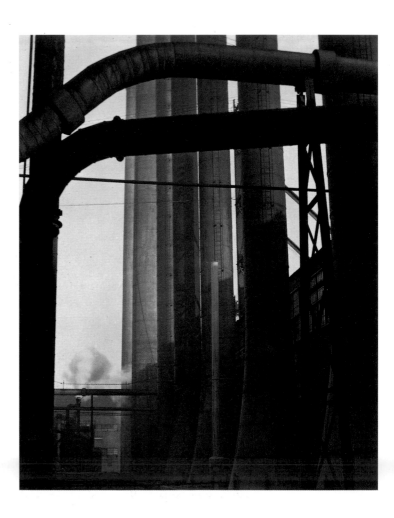

POSITIVE   See NEGATIVE.

PRINT:
LATER, MODERN,
POSTHUMOUS, VINTAGE,
COPY

Because a photographic print made close to the date of its negative, by or under the direct supervision of the photographer, is thought to most clearly capture the photographer's original inspiration, it is usually the most sought-after print of any from that negative. In commerce, such photographs are often called vintage prints. A modern or later print is made from the original negative, presumably by the photographer, but at a later date than that of the negative and perhaps employing different printing papers than those of earlier prints. A posthumous print is a print made from an original negative after the death of the photographer. A copy print is made from a new negative taken of an original print and usually has negligible value as a collectible object, except, perhaps, when the photographer uses the copying process for an aesthetic purpose.

PRINTING-OUT PAPER

Printing-out paper was designed for the production of a photographic print from a negative by the action of light alone on light-sensitive material, rather than by development using chemicals (see also DEVELOPING-OUT paper). Although ALBUMEN prints were printed out, the term *printing-out paper* (p.o.p.) is reserved for those commercially manufactured papers coated with silver-chloride emulsions, usually made of gelatin but sometimes of COLLODION, that were in general use, particularly for portraiture, from the 1880s until the late 1920s. The paper was exposed in contact with a negative until the image was wholly visible. No chemical development followed, simply WASHING and TONING. After 1900, p.o.p. gradually gave way to developing-out paper. As the printing-out process required the continual use of the negative, a second print could not be started until the first was completed. Fewer prints could be produced in a day than with the developing-out process, in which the negative was necessary only for the initial segment of the process. Photographs made on printing-out paper exhibit warm image tones and can have a wide variety of surfaces from glossy to matte.

RECTO/VERSO

The recto of a photograph is the side bearing the image, the front, as opposed to the verso, the back. If the photograph is mounted to another sheet of paper or other support, the verso is the back of the mount.

RETOUCHING

The careful manual alteration of the appearance of a print or negative is called retouching. It is most often used in portraiture to make cosmetic improvements to a sitter's appearance, such as removing minor facial blemishes, softening outlines or wrinkles, or "powdering" shining noses. It can also be a far more extensive correction of perceived defects in the print. Intrusive backgrounds can be muted or removed, as can extraneous compositional details. Values can be strengthened or weakened or elements added, as when clouds were painted into nineteenth-century landscapes with overexposed skies. The common tools for retouching are scalpels, perfectly pointed brushes, airbrushes, and retouching pencils. The materials are watercolors, inks, retouching dyes, and chemical reducers, akin to bleaches. See also SPOTTING.

SABATTIER EFFECT

See SOLARIZATION.

SALT PRINT
(SALTED-PAPER PRINT)

Salt prints, the earliest positive prints, were normally made by CONTACT PRINTING, usually from paper negatives (CALOTYPES) but occasionally from COLLODION negatives on glass. Invented by William Henry Fox Talbot in 1840, salt prints were a direct outgrowth of his earlier PHOTOGENIC DRAWING process. A salt print was made by sensitizing a sheet of paper in a solution of salt (sodium chloride) and then coating it on one side only with silver nitrate. Light-sensitive silver chloride was thus formed in the paper. After drying, the paper was put sensitive side up directly beneath a negative under a sheet of glass in a printing frame. This paper-negative-glass sandwich was exposed, glass side up, outdoors in sunlight, i.e., it was contact printed. The length of exposure, up to two hours, was determined by visual inspection. When the print had reached the desired intensity it was removed from the frame and fixed with sodium thiosulfate, at that time called hyposulfite of soda ("hypo"), which stopped the chemical reactions. It was then thoroughly washed and dried. The print could be toned with gold chloride for greater permanence and richer tone. A finished salt print is matte in tone, reddish brown in color, and has no surface gloss. If toned, it is purplish brown; if faded, yellowish brown. Its highlights are usually white. Salt prints were made until about 1860, although in decreasing numbers after the advent of the ALBUMEN print in 1851.

Occasionally salt prints were varnished with a thin coating of albumen to produce a somewhat glossy surface. Such prints have been referred to as albumenized salt prints.

It was also possible, as Louis-Desiré Blanquart-Evrard announced in 1851, to make a salt print by a quicker method than printing it out. The print could be briefly exposed under the negative and developed in the same way as a negative, then FIXED and WASHED. This method, which is less dependent than contact printing on continuous strong natural light, made possible the making of many prints from a single negative within a single day. It produced a salt print that was matte in tone, without surface gloss, and neutral in color, i.e., black, gray, and white, sometimes with bluish gray undertones. In short, Blanquart-Evrard's process involved initial contact printing, then DEVELOPING OUT; Talbot's called for continuous contact printing (PRINTING OUT).

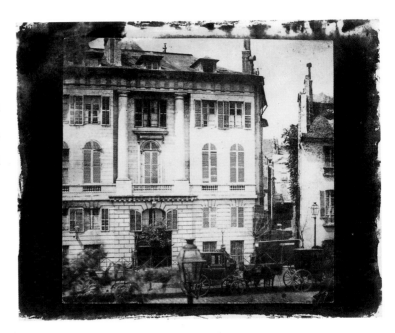

SALT PRINT
(SALTED-PAPER PRINT)
William Henry Fox Talbot
(British, 1800–1877)
Carriages and Parisian Town
Houses, 1843
Salt print with untrimmed
edges from a paper
negative (calotype)
Image: 16.8 × 17.3 cm
(6⅝ × 6¹³⁄₁₆ in.)
Sheet: 19 × 23 cm
(7½ × 9¹⁄₁₆ in.)
JPGM
84.XM.478.6

SENSITIVITY

Sensitivity is the capacity of responding to light that gives SILVER SALTS (silver halides), some iron salts, and bichromated colloids (such as gum bichromate) their photographic utility. To enable or enhance that capacity to chemically or physically change by the action of light is to sensitize a material so that a photographic image can be generated. The method of sensitizing varies by photographic process.

SHUTTER

See APERTURE.

SILVER-BROMIDE PRINT
/SILVER-CHLORIDE PRINT

See GELATIN SILVER PRINT.

Silver print

This is a shorthand term for what should be called a GELATIN SILVER print, meaning a paper coated with a gelatin emulsion containing SILVER SALTS. The term should be avoided because most black-and-white photographic prints contain silver, and the term is therefore too inclusive to be useful.

Silver salts

Silver salts are chemical compounds formed by the combination of silver with chlorine, bromine, and iodine, collectively called the halogens, to form silver chloride, silver bromide, and silver iodide. These three, the silver halides or silver salts, are crystalline in form and are sensitive to light, that is, they react to light by darkening. Each halide reacts at a different speed. These salts, alone or in combination, when coated on paper or film can be placed in a camera and, when exposed to light directed to the paper by a lens, produce a photographic negative. They are also present in the materials from which positives, commonly called prints, are made. The means by which the halides are formed or the way they are attached to the film or paper varies with each of the photographic processes. (See also CALOTYPE, SALT print, COLLODION, ALBUMEN print, and GELATIN SILVER print.) In processing, the silver halides are converted by chemical means to metallic silver. Silver salts are thus the basis of most photographic chemistry.

Snapshot

This term applies to an informal and apparently unposed and instantaneous photograph, usually made by an amateur, without artistic intention and as a keepsake of persons, places, or events.

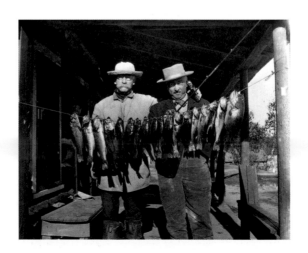

Snapshot
Unknown maker
American School
Fishermen and Their Catch
c. 1900
Gelatin silver print
9.9 × 12.1 cm
(3⅞ × 4¾ in.)
JPGM
84.XA.1537.36

Although the term *solarization* has come to be used to describe the Sabattier effect, in fact the partial reversals of tone in photographic prints to which both terms refer are differently caused. True solarization occurs when an intense light source, like the sun, is visible in a photograph that has been extremely overexposed in the camera, usually accidentally. The overexposure causes the light source to appear dark in the print. The sun becomes a black disk, but the reversal of tones is limited to this area of the print.

The Sabattier effect, named for Armand Sabattier (1834–1910), who discovered it in 1862, is an intentional darkroom technique, employed to produce tone reversals. The procedure is to partially develop a negative *or* print, momentarily expose it to light, then continue the normal development process. Tone reversal in completed prints principally occurs in background dark areas, which become appreciably lighter. At edges, between areas of the print where reversal has occurred and where it has not, a distinct black line is visible, particularly if it was the negative rather than the developing print that was flashed with light. Results of the Sabattier effect are somewhat unpredictable.

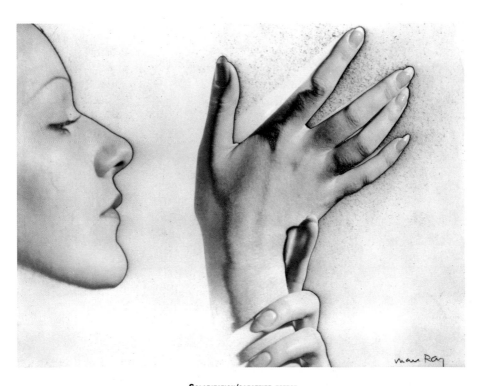

SOLARIZATION/SABATTIER EFFECT
Man Ray (American, 1890–1976). *Profile and Hands*, 1932.
Gelatin silver print showing Sabattier effect, 18×22.9 cm (7 ¹⁄₁₆×9 in.). JPGM, 84.XM.839.5.

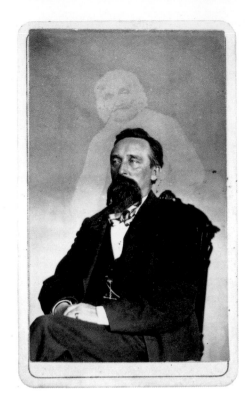

SPIRIT PHOTOGRAPH
William H. Mumler
(American, 1832–1884)
John J. Glover
with Spirit of Old Woman
Hovering Above Him
c. 1862
Albumen print
carte-de-visite
9.6 × 5.7 cm
(3¾ × 2¼ in.)
JPGM
84.XD.760.1.6

SPIRIT PHOTOGRAPH

In the nineteenth century, a ghostly figure was sometimes included alongside or above the sitter in a portrait in order to convey the impression that a spirit was present. Spirit photographs were usually made by having the person playing the spirit remain in view only briefly during the long exposure of a negative. The hoax being perpetrated in a spirit photograph was that photography could capture images of the dead or departed, particularly if the sitter thought about the absent person. See also GHOST.

SPOTTING

Spotting is a specialized kind of RETOUCHING used to fill accidental pinholes in a negative or, more often, to darken minute white spots on a print, often caused by dust on the negative. When a photograph has faded, the spotting sometimes remains darker, giving an idea of the image's original tonality and color.

STEREOGRAPH

A stereograph is a pair of photographic images on a single support that, when viewed through a stereoscope designed to hold it, gives the appearance of a single image having relief and solidity, that is, being in three dimensions. A standard stereograph consists of a piece of stiff card, often highly colored, from 3½ to 4½ inches (8.9 to 11.4 cm) tall and about 7 inches (17.8 cm) wide, to which two photographs, generally ALBUMEN prints, each 3 to 4½ inches (7.6 to 11.4 cm) high and about 3 inches (7.6 cm) wide, have been mounted next to each other. Remaining space on the front of the card usually bears the photographer's and/or publisher's name(s) and a title, as does the back of the card. The photographs are not identical but exhibit a slight lateral shift, having been made with a dual-lens camera, the centers of the lenses being set the same distance apart (2½ inches [6.3 cm]) as the centers of two human eyes. Each photograph is thus an image of what one eye would see. When viewed through the stereoscope the two images combine, approximating human binocular vision. In order to convey the illusion of depth, a strong foreground is desirable. Viewing stereographs was a vastly popular parlor amusement from the mid-1850s well into the twentieth century. Stereographic subjects vary widely, although topographical views are perhaps most common.

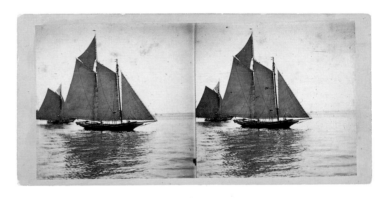

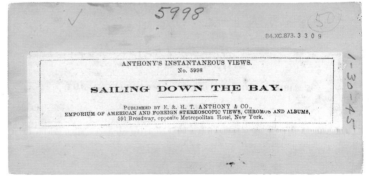

STEREOGRAPH
Edward and
Henry T. Anthony
(American, 1819–1888,
1814–1884)
Sailing Down the Bay, 1869
Albumen print
stereograph
7.4 × 15.4 cm
(2 ¹⁵⁄₁₆ × 6 ¹⁄₁₆ in.)
JPGM
84.XC.873.3309
recto and verso

TALBOTYPE   See CALOTYPE.

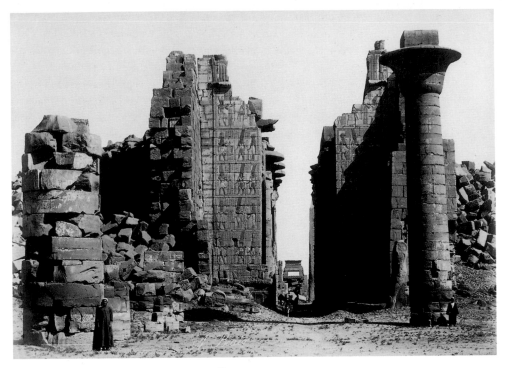

TINTED PHOTOGRAPH
Antonio Beato (Italian, c. 1825–1903). *First Court of the Temple of Karnak*, c. 1885.
Rose-tinted albumen print, 26×36 cm (10¼×14³⁄₁₆ in.). JPGM, 84.XM.1382.55.

TINTED PHOTOGRAPH

A tinted photograph has a single overall color resulting from the addition of dyes to the photographic materials by a commercial manufacturer. The color is suffused throughout and most visible in the highlights and midtones. ALBUMEN printing papers in pale pink or blue were available from the 1870s onward, as were GELATIN-SILVER PRINTING-OUT papers in pale mauve or pink from the 1890s onward. Other kinds of tinted papers also existed. Such coloration is now often very faded. Tinted photographs are to be distinguished from HAND-COLORED or TONED photographs in which the image itself has color because of the individual photographer's manipulations.

TINTYPE
(FERROTYPE)

The ferrotype, better known as the tintype in America where it reached its greatest popularity, was derived from the AMBROTYPE and like it depended on the fact that a COLLODION negative appeared to be a positive image when viewed against a dark background. In the case of the tintype the negative was made not on glass but on a thin sheet of iron coated with an opaque black or chocolate-brown lacquer or enamel. (As the tintype was iron rather than tin, *tintype* is a misnomer.) The lacquered sheet, which was commercially available, was coated with wet collodion containing SILVER SALTS just before exposure in the camera. Development immediately followed exposure. Later refinements led to the use of a dry-collodion-coated metal plate. As the finished image was in fact, although not in appearance, a negative, the image was usually laterally reversed. A tintype was a unique image and could only be duplicated by being rephotographed. Despite the image reversal, tintypes were almost always used for portraiture. From their origin in the 1850s until the end of the century and beyond, they remained popular because they were very inexpensive. Like daguerreotypes or ambrotypes, tintypes were sometimes placed in small folding cases (see CASED PHOTOGRAPHS), but more often they were inserted into simple folding cards or window mats, sometimes made of thin metal. Most tintypes have very limited tonal ranges and appear flat and soft by comparison with either a daguerreotype or an ambrotype. Tintypes were often made by street vendors.

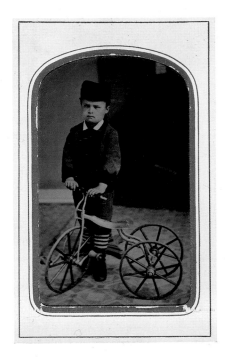

TINTYPE
(FERROTYPE)
Unknown maker
American School
Boy with Tricycle, c. 1870
Ferrotype (in its folder)
7.6 × 4.5 cm
(3 × 1¾ in.)
JPGM
84.XT.1395.78

TONING

Toning denotes a variety of means available for changing or shifting the color of the image of a photographic print. Its use is largely governed by aesthetic choice on the part of the photographer, but toning with certain compounds, notably gold chloride or platinum salts, also enhances image stability (and thus the permanence of the print) and usually increases contrast. Gold toning, the most common means in the nineteenth century, originated in the daguerrean era, and since then each photographic process has had specific toning procedures to produce specific hues. Selenium toning prevails today. Toning can occur in the course of development, or after development in subsidiary steps in which the silver comprising the image is chemically altered or partially replaced by another metal. After development, the image can be bleached in a solution containing a mordant (a substance capable of absorbing dye) and then dyed. The number of variables in any of these procedures is large. In development toning, the original chemical composition of the print, the temperature, composition, and strength of the developer, the length of development, and the means of drying the print all affect the final tone. In postdevelopment toning, in which the silver is altered, bleached, or replaced, the choice of toning solutions is wide, including those containing sulfur or, most frequently, one of the following metals: gold, iron, copper, uranium, mercury, platinum, palladium, vanadium, or selenium. The range of possible tones is concomitantly wide, including warm browns, purples, sepias, blues, olives, red-browns, and blue-blacks. In toning by dyeing after bleaching there is a choice from a virtually unlimited spectrum of image colors.

A toned photograph should be distinguished from a TINTED or HAND-COLORED one.

TRIMMING　　　　See CROPPING.

VAN DYKE PRINT　　See KALLITYPE.

VARIANT　　　　A variant is an image that is very closely related to, but not the same as, a known image, as when a photographer makes a second, horizontal, photograph of a still life that was first photographed in a vertical format, without significantly changing lighting or exposure and, presumably, during the same studio session. A variant may also occur when a photographer prints the same negative twice but chooses to markedly alter tonalities or contrast. (With modern cameras, roll film, and frequent exposures, the potential for variants has multiplied, but the photographer must choose to print the two versions of an image to create an actual variant.)

VERSO　　　　　See RECTO.

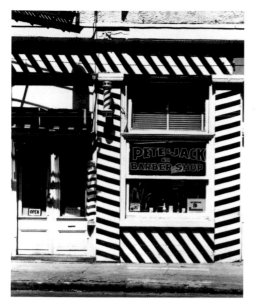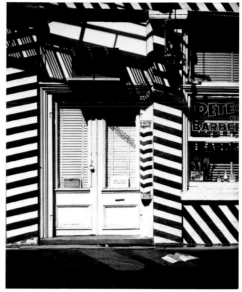

VARIANT

Ralston Crawford (American, 1906–1978). *Barbershop, New Orleans*, 1960.
Gelatin silver print, 60.7×51 cm (23⅞×20⅟₁₆ in.). JPGM, 84.XM.151.158.
Pete and Jack's Barbershop, 1960. Gelatin silver print, 24.7×19.8 cm (9¾×7¹³⁄₁₆ in.). JPGM, 84.XM.151.121.

VIEW CAMERA
(FIELD CAMERA)

This imprecise American term is roughly equivalent to the British
term FIELD CAMERA and is applied to cameras meant for making
relatively large-scale negatives, particularly of outdoor scenes.
It often refers to nineteenth-century cameras that required
tripods and utilized glass plates that were necessarily exposed one
at a time and CONTACT PRINTED rather than ENLARGED. View
cameras had a variety of means for altering the relation of the
lens to the position of the negative. In the twentieth century, such
cameras are often used for architectural studies, advertising and
commercial work, and sometimes for work in the field. A view
camera is the opposite of a MINIATURE CAMERA.

VIGNETTE

A vignette is a photograph in which a central image dissolves into
a surrounding ground, nearly always a field of white. Oval vignet-
ting was popular in nineteenth-century portraiture and was
accomplished by photographing the subject through an opaque
mask with an oval opening placed close to the lens or, more
frequently, by printing the negative through a similar mask with
partially translucent inner edges. (The term is sometimes ill-
advisedly used to describe the unintentional effect in nineteenth-
century photographs created when an image falls off at its corners

under a negative of the image to be reproduced. (The talc under-coating facilitated the separation of the film from the glass.) After the portion of the gelatin that had not hardened had been washed away, the tough gelatin mold was squeezed under very heavy pressure into a sheet of soft lead, producing a reversed mold that could be used for printing. After greasing, the lead mold was filled with pigmented gelatin, usually a rich purple-brown in color, and a sheet of paper was placed on it. In a hand press, the gelatin was forcibly transferred to the paper, the excess gelatin being forced out around the edges of the mold. Removed from the press, the gelatin contracted and flattened as it dried. The inky edges were trimmed away and the print mounted. The tonal scale of the resultant image in pigmented gelatin was very true to the original, and the image was highly luminous. Unlike other photomechanical processes, a Woodburytype, called a photo-glyptie by the French, has continuous tone, showing neither a screen nor a grain pattern. Woodburytypes are usually labeled as such.

WOODBURYTYPE
(PHOTOGLYPTIE)
John Thomson
(British, 1837–1921)
Covent Garden
Flower Women, 1877
Woodburytype
9 × 8.5 cm
(4¾ × 3⅜ in.)
JPGM
84.XB.1361.3

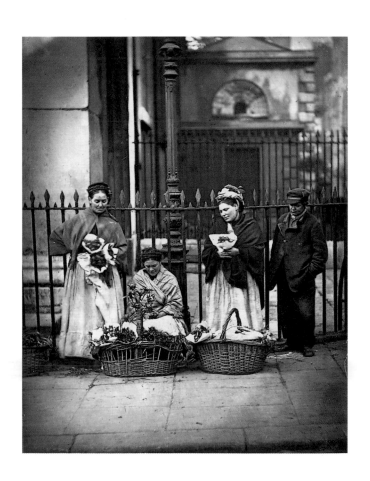

Selected Bibliography

The bibliography that follows is confined to a few twentieth-century works that are particularly helpful and generally available in reference libraries. It does not include the nineteenth- and early twentieth-century manuals that were extensively consulted in the writing of this book.

TECHNICAL

Coe, Brian, and Mark Haworth-Booth. *A Guide to Early Photographic Processes*. London, 1983.

Crawford, William. *The Keepers of Light: A History and Working Guide to Early Photographic Processes*. Dobbs Ferry, N.Y., 1979.

Focal Encyclopedia of Photography. New York, 1969.

International Center of Photography. *Encyclopedia of Photography*. New York, 1984.

Jones, Bernard E., ed. *Cassell's Encyclopedia of Photography*. 2 vols. New York, 1912.

Macauley, David. *The Way Things Work*. Boston, 1988.

Nadeau, Luis. *Encyclopedia of Printing, Photographic, and Photomechanical Processes*. 2 vols. Fredericton, New Brunswick, 1989 and 1990.

Reilly, James M. *Care and Identification of Nineteenth-Century Photographic Prints*. Rochester, N.Y., 1986.

Stroebel, Leslie, et al. *Photographic Materials and Processes*. Boston, 1986.

HISTORICAL

Bernard, Bruce, and Valerie Lloyd. *Photodiscovery: Masterworks of Photography, 1840–1940*. New York, 1980.

Goldschmidt, Lucien, and Weston Naef. *The Truthful Lens: A Survey of the Photographically Illustrated Book*. New York, 1980.

Greenough, Sarah, et al. *On the Art of Fixing a Shadow*. Washington, D.C., 1989.

Naef, Weston. *The Collection of Alfred Stieglitz: Fifty Pioneers of Modern Photography*. New York, 1978.

Newhall, Beaumont. *The History of Photography*. New York, 1982.

Rosenblum, Naomi. *A World History of Photography*. New York, 1984.

Szarkowski, John. *Photography Until Now*. New York, 1989.

Weaver, Mike, ed. *The Art of Photography*. London, 1989.

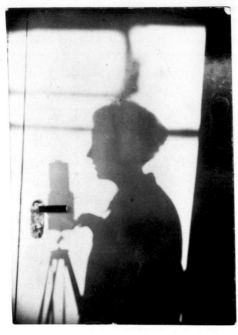

Charlotte (Lotte) Beese (German, 1903–1988). *Self-Portrait*, 1927.
Gelatin silver print, 8.4 × 5.9 cm (3⁵/₁₆ × 2¹⁵/₁₆ in.). JPGM, 85.XP.384.79.

Project staff:

John Harris, Editor

Kurt Hauser, Designer

Eric Kassouf, Production Coordinator

Stephenie Blakemore, Charles Passela, Ellen Rosenbery,

Jack Ross, Photographers

Robin Clark, Publications Intern

Thea Piegdon, Production Artist

Typeset by Wilsted & Taylor, Oakland, California

Printed by L. E. G. O., SpA, Vicenza, Italy